GATHERINGS

GATHERINGS

Recipes for feasts great and small

FLORA SHEDDEN

MITCHELL BEAZLEY

TO MUMMA,
FOR EVERYTHING

An Hachette UK Company
www.hachette.co.uk

First published in Great Britain
in 2017 by Mitchell Beazley,
a division of Octopus
Publishing Group Ltd
Carmelite House
50 Victoria Embankment
London EC4Y 0DZ
www.octopusbooks.co.uk

Distributed in the US by
Hachette Book Group
1290 Avenue of the Americas
4th and 5th Floors
New York, NY 10020

Distributed in Canada by
Canadian Manda Group
664 Annette St. Toronto,
Ontario, Canada M6S 2C8

ISBN 978 1 78472 219 7

A CIP catalogue record for this book
is available from the British Library.

Printed and bound in China

10 9 8 7 6 5 4 3 2 1

Editorial Director: Eleanor Maxfield
Managing Editor: Sybella Stephens
Copy Editor: Salima Hirani
Senior Designer: Jaz Bahra
Photographer: Laura Edwards
Food Stylist: Annie Rigg
Props Stylist: Tabitha Hawkins
Production Manager: Caroline Alberti

CONTENTS

INTRODUCTION

I have spent my whole life in the kitchen. I don't recall a single week in my 20 years during which I haven't cooked or at least attempted to. From offering to stir and pour things at a young age, to serving hearty plates of pasta, some sort of elaborate sponge or even knocking up a simple salad, I have always found myself padding about the kitchen barefoot and occasionally donning an apron. It's not coincidental that food is in my nature. My mother is an excellent cook, her mother is an excellent cook, my dad's mother is an excellent cook, my aunties are excellent cooks, my cousins are excellent cooks. It was an inescapable fate. The position I am in now, however, was less than expected. Food was never considered as a career path, not even for a minute. I remember, aged 15, when tentatively broaching the "what on earth shall I do with my life?" subject, my mum declared I was definitely not to go into catering, a business, she described as thankless and brutally exhausting, having worked as a cook for years. I spent all my weekends from the age of 13 waitressing in various cafés, and occasionally helping Mum out with weddings or parties in the evenings, so I was well aware of the hours of graft that go into it. I knew she was right and set off to meet a careers advisor to talk all things academic.

Cooking remained a hobby, and when I left home to study architecture in Edinburgh, I am willing to bet I was the only student who arrived with nine cake tins, four spatulas, a paella pan, my mixer and enough ingredients to fill every cupboard in the flat. A year in, I was left uninspired, spending more money and time at farmers' markets and restaurants than I was in the library and, if I am honest, pubs and clubs. I returned home during the spring exam period feeling quite heartbroken that it had not been the dream I had anticipated. My cookbook collection had doubled but, alas, I was not to be the next Zaha Hadid.

I moped about the kitchen for a month or so, cooking and eating obscene quantities of food and thoroughly irritating my parents and sisters. Then one Tuesday, late at night and in a state of panic, I emailed a local gallery and asked for a job. I have since re-read the somewhat desperate email to my great embarrassment. Hugh the gallery owner did, however, agree to meet me and a week later I was helping hang an exhibition. I stayed at the lovely Frames Gallery in Perth for a year and a half, establishing a happy routine of working, food shopping and spending any time off in the kitchen. It was at Frames that I began my blog. I was doing a semi-grown-up job, feeding my family and saving (a little) money while the rest of my friends were running wild at university. It was a little isolating if I am truthful, and so I settled on the idea of my own wee project. I am a very visual person in all elements of my life, and having spent hours decorating bakes or styling food just so, I wanted to do a decent job when it came to pictures of my food. I saved up for a month and bought myself an old wedding photographer's camera off eBay. After that, florashedden.com was born, and I was thrilled to have an excuse to cook and share plates and bakes slightly more adventurous than my then ten-year-old sister's palette. It has very much been a learning curve, but I love having a wee space on the internet to natter ridiculously about exceptionally good-looking radicchio, or some cookies that had turned out well 217 attempts later. It was at this time that I discovered people actually do have and enjoy careers in food, careers that don't solely depend on doing two days' prep, a manic flurry of service, then 7 tonnes of dishes at 3am. There were jobs for home cooks that relished in nothing more than pottering, experimenting and styling. I was delighted by this well-kept secret.

Early in January 2015 I stumbled upon a second secret. I had submitted a form to a small baking show on the BBC. It occurred only after many friends and family members had sent me links to the applications page, some even printing off copies for me. My middle sister, Hebe, punched me on the arm multiple times. I succumbed 4 hours and 37 minutes before the deadline and sent off my long-winded and, in hindsight, cringe-worthy answers and images. I received a call from a London number three days later. Many stages followed, including a trip to Manchester with my dad driving and me sporadically shouting "The cake!" when he took a sharp corner. There was also a snowstorm at Gatwick when I was due to land early one Saturday for a final audition, meaning I practically ran to a kitchen in Hackney, arriving flustered, sweaty and two hours late. Somehow, somewhere in this chaos, I found myself in a hotel in sleepy Newbury one April evening being introduced to cast and crew.

I spent the next nine weeks trekking up and down the country, exhausted, often in a sugar coma and regularly cursing my poor judgement on éclairs and custards. The ironic thing was that I spent more time cooking than I did baking prior to this bizarre *Bake Off* turn of events. I try not to spend too much time reflecting, but I would like to say a huge thank you to everyone at Love Productions, the lovely crew that never failed to make me laugh, the bakers for being as loony as I was and thinking no one would watch and all the viewers who watched each week despite our car-crash-baking and general madness. My fondest memories are of people coming up to me in supermarkets, on the street, in cafés, shops and cinemas only to say a hello. And to everyone on social media, I adored seeing your pictures, hearing about parties, your granny's comments on a certain male judge and your general well wishes. I loved meeting and speaking to every single one of you, and had it not been for your kind natures, I wouldn't be sitting here, wrapped in a blanket, blethering about food late into the night. Thank you.

Post-cakes, bakes and reality telly, my cooking style has noticeably changed. I moved to the coast, for a start, and I desperately craved a return to savoury. Fish became a regular feature as a result of my flat sitting right on the glorious St Andrews harbour. In fact, the majority of this book has been written while intermittently watching the tide, the boats, the surfers, the dog walkers and the late-night couples go about their business. I got to know the lovely local fishermen, too, who have provided me with the best fish and seafood I have ever feasted on. And I have spent more time cooking for others than I ever have before. It had been an intense year and I was desperate to catch up with friends I had neglected, family I had missed and generally gather round the kitchen table for a good old natter. I made big, colourful salads, cooked joints of meat for hours and hours, fried, roasted and braised my way through everything edible and occasionally returned to baking for a wee sponge to enjoy mid-afternoon on a wet, windy day. And so when the question of a book came about, I knew I wanted to write about cooking for others.

Food for me is an excuse to gather people – for at least one meal a day, when you can sit, socialize and share stories about your day, or about others. It isn't just about eating, it is all the things that come with that process: passing the bread, tales that come when someone is a little over-tipsy, sticky fingers, dishes that remind guests of previously visited places or anecdotes. It is as much about fuelling as it is about good hearty laughs. Cooking is the rewarding route you take to get there.

"So what is the plan for tonight?"
"Nothing complicated – just a wee gathering"

A gathering is an easy way of hosting: it means there is no pressure, no code of conduct and everyone – cook included – can actually enjoy themselves. For my age group particularly, dinner makes us think of something formal, involved and maybe even exhausting. A gathering is the opposite. I wanted to reflect this relaxed style of eating in a collection of easy and accessible recipes that are not daunting but enticing and encouraging to those of us who want to have people over, make supper or lay on a spread without sliding into full-on panic mode. Those who want to create something that will echo the mood, something humble, yet appetizing, and delicious. What's more, I wanted to show how this is all possible after a long day at work, after a weekend spent out and about or even after decking the halls.

I am from the generation with arguably the most delusional approach to food. We were born when all sorts of chemical-based and processed snacks and meals were the norm, but soon the scaremongering came and we were told to say no to most additives, E numbers and the like. Suddenly, at the age of five, I was asking Mum things like "Is there any MSG in these?" or "Are they organic?". We were terrified – and so were our parents. I have been fortunate enough never to have experienced a troubled relationship with food, principally due to having an excellent and stubborn mother. I have, however, been very close to people less lucky and seen first-hand how earth-shattering eating disorders are. At the age of 14, a boy told me "don't even consider eating that bagel". I had just been in PE and it would apparently counteract any physical exercise I had just done, and I would therefore gain a million stones there and then. This is a daunting prospect for a teen attempting to find a normal approach to food.

When I browse bookshop shelves nowadays, I am often surprised by the sheer number of juicing, carb-cutting and sugar-free "cookbooks" on offer, the majority of which are brought to you by authors of a similar age to myself. In a world already cluttered with lifestyle contradictions, it worries me that people so young can easily read and follow such a drastic diet change. I have no training in this field and cannot promise nutritional science or calorie-counting, but I can promise common-sense food – proper and honest ingredients that will both fuel and satisfy you. I am not on a mission, and I am certainly not one to preach, but I would urge everyone – from those stepping into the kitchen for the first time to those simply trying to fix something for dinner – to consider just how sensible cutting entire food groups from your diet can actually be. Life is a balancing act and your dinner plate shouldn't be any different.

This book contains recipes for what I believe to be a mixture of balanced modern dishes, staple snacks, salads and sides, interesting bakes and puddings perfect to end a meal with. Nothing overly fussy or complicated, just tasty and pretty plates of food. This book, I hope, reflects the fact that there is a huge surge in the amount of people young and old who want to eat proper food off real plates in good company. Ultimately, I feel cooking should be about beautiful yet affordable and achievable dishes, and this was my aim with these recipes. I give you a mixture of ideas for your gatherings small and large, those planned out in advance or assembled at the very last minute, and those that are remembered long after the washing-up is done. Now to set the table…

With love,

Flora
Scotland, 2017

HOW TO USE THIS BOOK

I am not a chef. With the exception of one long, sweaty summer's day, I have never worked in a professional restaurant, nor have I ever cooked anything sous vide, or used those scary and wildly efficient blenders all chefs seem to have. There is no stainless steel present in my kitchen, nor are there seven willing pot-washers waiting for the dishes (unfortunately). I am a home cook, with skills no greater than most others up and down the country. These recipes are not flashy or difficult, nor are they expensive or time-consuming. They simply offer a way of sharing ideas I have discovered while playing around in the kitchen, combinations I have found particularly tasty and even passing on the classics that I was taught to make at a young age. The vast majority of these recipes are simple, containing only a few key ingredients and processes. More importantly, they should be life-friendly. Below are some tips.

Before beginning a recipe, try as much as possible to do the following:

* Gather your ingredients together and have them close to hand. I have burnt, ruined and completely forgotten about things while rummaging in badly organized cupboards for ingredients I don't even know whether I have or not.

* Have a clutter-free work surface. I am the queen of clutter and very rarely follow this rule, but it really does minimize kitchen chaos and helps to achieve a more successful end result.

* Make sure your equipment is clean and ready to go. It sounds obvious, but having to muddle through a sink full of dishes halfway through making a cake is never ideal.

* Read the recipe in full. This is a tip that lovely Mary Berry shared with us every day in the tent, and one that, though simple, should never be ignored.

Be prepared to improvise. The most important thing I want you to know about this book is that it will welcome substitutions with open arms. If you don't like broccoli, by all means use kale instead; if the idea of passion fruit terrifies you, top your pudding with something else, such as raspberries or mango; if you cannot conceive of anything worse than a green olive tapenade, use black olives, or omit completely and search for another side dish, either in the pages of this book or another. Make the recipes your own and please do not be precious. If you spend every minute in the kitchen panicked about correct ingredients, you will not enjoy your time there. The results will change, but change does not at all mean that the end dish will be bad. Simply put, I offer you some flavour ideas – run with them if you like. Tweak them as you see fit.

I am definitely not reinventing the wheel here, or even a way of eating for that matter, but what I do hope for is that you find this book inspiring and encouraging, no matter how afraid you are of the kitchen. And I hope more than anything that it makes you call your friends and invite them round for dinner.

HOW TO SET THE TABLE

This book is chock-a-block with dishes and recipes designed for sharing. I love to plonk big platters on the table and get folks to help themselves. A gathering should be as much about a gathering of people as a gathering of dishes. You are creating a spread that will invite people to the table on its own. It should be encouraging, enticing and even a little exciting.

For this you will need some beautiful big platters and dishes to serve your food on. This may seem like a luxury, and it is in no way essential, but it is well worth spending a little money on. Look in charity and antiques shops for platters and dishes if you like that style, or in supermarkets or large homeware stores for cheaper and more modern versions. I also suggest getting a few large bowls fit for salads, fruits and veggies. Other good tableware includes small glass bottles or jars for dressings, ceramic jugs for gravies and sauces, big wooden boards that can be used for both chopping and serving, a large glass jug for water or drinks and a few mats or tiles to protect the surface of the table from hot oven-to-table dishes. In terms of cutlery, I don't believe you need to go to the faff of laying it out. Leave it in a pile or a tin and let people grab it themselves. I would recommend having some big spoons, salad servers and maybe even a set of tongs to hand. A bunch of nice paper napkins are also really, really useful for guests – you can, by all means, go for linen ones if you are feeling fancy.

The one thing I would say is worth the expense is a nice bunch of fresh flowers that you can cut and make into sweet wee posies to run down the centre of the table (no one wants a big bunch slap bang in the middle that you can't see over). And a few tea lights will do no harm at all.

ESSENTIAL EQUIPMENT

Below is a list of the kit I adore and use almost daily. You can get such a variety of affordable utensils nowadays and could probably deck out your kitchen for the same price as a posh meal out. It will aid your culinary adventures tenfold. If you are just starting out please do consider acquiring all of the below, but don't rush into it, as I know it is a big list. A good workman never blames his tools, but it helps if he has the right ones.

* 2 wooden chopping boards (1 sweet, 1 savoury; and make sure you have a specific side for onions and garlic – no one wants toast and jam with a garlicky tang)
* 2–3 mixing bowls in various sizes
* measuring jug
* fine sieve
* colander (preferably metal so that it can double up as a steamer)
* 2–3 wooden spoons (1 sweet, 1 savoury)
* ladle
* spatula (get a few)
* fish slice
* vegetable peeler
* garlic crusher
* wooden rolling pin
* pastry brush (I use one designed for watercolour paints, as it has softer bristles)
* whisk

* grater
* small serrated knife (often called a tomato knife; I couldn't live without my Victorinox one – inexpensive and indispensable)
* sharp butcher's or chef's knife
* bread knife
* butter knife or small metal spatula (round-ended)
* 3 saucepans in various sizes (2 with lids, preferably)
* large ovenproof casserole dish (cast iron or ceramic)
* griddle pan
* nonstick frying pan
* deep roasting tray
* baking tray
* 20cm (8 inch) round loose-bottomed cake tin
* food processor
* stick blender
* electric whisk or stand mixer

A GOOD LARDER

Here's a list of the food items I always keep in the fridge, freezer or cupboard. When I use up any of these items, I make sure they are replaced the next time I go shopping.

* good sea salt flakes (I use Maldon) and freshly ground black peppercorns
* extra virgin olive oil (for dressings)
* olive oil (for cooking)
* lemons (I use them by the bucketful; I read recently about a campaign for them to become a third seasoning, after salt and pepper – I fully back this)
* limes (great for Asian dishes and, more importantly, G&Ts)
* white wine vinegar
* balsamic vinegar
* soy sauce
* both Dijon and grainy mustard
* a good chutney
* fresh herbs (see page 23)
* fresh chilli
* fennel seeds
* caraway seeds
* coriander seeds
* yellow mustard seeds
* ground cumin
* ground turmeric
* smoked paprika
* bay leaves
* sumac
* saffron threads
* clear honey
* vanilla bean paste

* pomegranate molasses
* green cardamom pods
* star anise
* whole nutmeg, for grating
* dark chocolate (preferably one with at least 54% cocoa solids)
* flours – plain, self-raising, rye and spelt
* sugars – caster, light brown, dark brown and demerara
* butter, unsalted
* ground coffee
* almonds – ground and flaked
* mixed seeds
* onions, white/banana shallots and red
* garlic
* canned beans and pulses
* canned chopped tomatoes
* tomato purée
* potatoes
* frozen peas
* stock – homemade or, alternatively, I like Marigold Vegetable Bouillon or Knorr Stock Pots
* pearl barley
* risotto or Arborio rice
* dried pasta (I like wholewheat spaghetti or tagliatelli)
* good rolled oats
* ice cubes

GROW YER OWN!

I am not suggesting moving to the country and living the good life. As a country girl myself, I know the hassle involved. What I am suggesting is that you pop to the supermarket and buy yourself a mixture of potted herbs (coriander, parsley, thyme, rosemary, basil and chives are all great). They are very inexpensive (you can get five to seven pots for less than a tenner) and are easy to store in the kitchen, taking up minimal space. In this book I call for a lot of fresh herbs, not because I am demanding, but because I really feel they can add to and lift most dishes. Using potted herbs is a far cheaper alternative, as all too often packets of fresh herbs are half used and then left to wilt at the back of the fridge. They will last as long as your memory docs – simply remember to give them a bit of water and TLC occasionally. I promise it will give both your food and your kitchen a vibrant kick of colour.

MORNINGS QUICK AND SLOW

My first attempt at granola was by candlelight in the depths of winter. Mid-power cut, I had the urge to bake, which was still an option despite the outage due to having an oil-fuelled AGA. What I hadn't factored in, however, was just how hard it is to tell if your granola is golden or not by tea light. That initial batch was very much overdone. When the electricity is on, I love to make trays and trays of the stuff, then bag it up with wee bows for gifts. This is a semi-healthy version, containing drastically less sugar or any of the nasties you would find in supermarket brands. It can be so easily adapted – please chop and change whatever you fancy with no fear. As long as the wet ingredients remain constant, you will be just fine. Serve the granola with good-quality yogurt and some berries or fresh figs.

FIG AND PUMPKIN SEED GRANOLA

MAKES APPROXIMATELY 750G (1LB 10OZ)

3 tablespoons coconut oil, at room temperature (i.e. in liquid form)
100ml (3½fl oz) maple syrup
100g (3½oz) clear honey
1 teaspoon vanilla bean paste
350g (12oz) rolled oats
50g (1¾oz) sesame seeds
25g (1oz) white poppy seeds (blue are fine if you can't get white)
100g (3½oz) pumpkin seeds
50g (1¾oz) flaked almonds
100g (3½oz) dried figs, roughly chopped
50g (1¾oz) coconut flakes

Preheat the oven to 160°C (325°F), Gas Mark 3.

Weigh out all the ingredients bar the figs and coconut flakes in a large bowl. Mix the lot together using your hands, ensuring everything is well coated in the wet ingredients.

Tip the mixture into a large roasting tray and bake for 10 minutes. Remove the tray from the oven and stir the granola around – this helps to ensure it colours evenly. Bake for a further 10 minutes or until golden and becoming crisp. (It will become crunchier once it cools down.) Add the figs and coconut flakes while the mixture is still hot and mix them through.

Allow the granola to cool completely, then package it up in a large jar or small cellophane gift bags. It will keep for about 1 month in airtight storage.

Believe it or not, I took inspiration for these bars from a Christmas cake recipe originally from New Zealand. Instead of the traditional dark, rich fruity number that hangs around for weeks post-Christmas, in this case the cake was lightly spiced, golden in colour and tropical in flavour. I adored it (partially due to the three different forms of alcohol involved) and wanted to create a way to enjoy its flavour all year round – these bars are the result. The ginger has the starring role here, so I don't recommend being mean with it. Wrap up a bar in greaseproof paper and chuck it in your bag for an on-the-go snack, or take a few with you on a picnic.

GOLDEN GLORY BARS

MAKES 10–12

350g (12oz) rolled oats

75g (2¾oz) mixed seeds (I use sesame, sunflower and white poppy seeds)

75g (2¾oz) ground almonds

100g (3½oz) dried apricots, chopped into small pieces

100g (3½oz) dried apple pieces, chopped into small pieces

50g (1¾oz) stem ginger, finely chopped

1 teaspoon ground ginger

150g (5½oz) unsalted butter, plus extra for greasing

150g (5½oz) clear honey

150g (5½oz) caster sugar

Preheat the oven to 160°C (325°F), Gas Mark 3. Grease and line a deep 23cm (9 inch) square baking tin with baking parchment or greaseproof paper.

Mix the oats, seeds, almonds, apricots, apple, stem ginger and ground ginger together in a large bowl.

Put the butter, honey and sugar into a saucepan and melt over a gentle heat until just combined. Pour this wet mixture over the dry mix, then stir well to coat the dry ingredients in the wet mix. Tip the combined mixture into your prepared tin and, using wet hands, press down firmly to flatten the surface.

Bake for 25–30 minutes or until golden on top. Allow to cool completely, then remove the slab from the tin and slice it into 10–12 bars. They will keep for up to 1 week in airtight storage.

Most mornings when at home, I am woken by my youngest sister, Willow, who is often describing the breakfast she would like me to prepare for her. A lot of the time it is pancakes, waffles or crêpes – the classics. Occasionally, she pushes the boat out and opts for a bostock or some nutmeg French toast. One time, however, she asked for porridge. I love porridge, really I do, but it was a sunny Sunday and I had plenty of time on my hands – of all the involved breakfasts I could make for her, she wanted porridge?! So I told her I would make toasted oats. We have not looked back since, and it is now the most requested breakfast item. It is ideal for the mornings you spend padding around barefoot and in your pyjamas with a never-ending pot of tea. It takes a little longer to cook compared to normal porridge but it is time well spent. Make sure you use proper rolled oats, not the quick-cook variety. The coconut is pretty tasty, but is not essential and can be easily substituted with flaked almonds, ground almonds or chopped pecans. If you want to avoid nuts, simply add more oats in place of the coconut and stir in some dried fruits such as dates or apricots when adding the liquid. Serve this tasty porridge with a dollop of yogurt and some seasonal fruit, or on its own with a little extra milk stirred in.

TOASTED COCONUT OATS

SERVES 4

knob of butter
125g (4½oz) rolled oats
50g (1¾oz) desiccated coconut
about 300ml (½ pint) water
300ml (½ pint) milk
25g (1oz) coconut sugar or
    soft light brown sugar
2 tablespoons agave nectar
pinch of salt

Put the butter into a medium saucepan and gently melt it over a low heat. Then increase the heat a little and add the oats and coconut. Stir for 3–4 minutes or until the oats are beginning to colour and the coconut has become fragrant.

In a jug, mix the water and milk together. Gradually add the liquid to the pan. Stir the mixture well between each addition and allow the liquid to be absorbed fully before adding more. (This is a very similar process to making a risotto.) Continue in this way for around 10–15 minutes until the oats are cooked through. (You may or may not need a little more water.)

Take the pan off the heat and stir in the sugar, agave nectar and salt. Serve the oats immediately.

I was given a waffle maker by my lovely Granny Joan on my 16th birthday. It came wrapped in the biggest bow you can imagine and left me grinning from ear to ear for weeks. I immediately went about experimenting with recipes, and this one is a favourite of mine.

RYE WAFFLES

MAKES 8–10

150g (5½oz) plain flour
150g (5½oz) rye flour
1 teaspoon baking powder
75g (2¾oz) caster sugar
3 eggs, lightly beaten
½ teaspoon ground cinnamon
300ml (½ pint) milk
100g (3½oz) unsalted butter, melted

To serve
whipped cream
Spiced Plum Compote (see page 262)

Preheat your waffle maker.

To make the batter, stir the flours, baking powder, sugar, eggs and cinnamon together, then whisk in the milk gradually. Continue to beat until the mixture is smooth. Finally, stir in the melted butter.

Ladle about 125ml (4fl oz) of the batter into the waffle iron and close the lid. Cook for 2–3 minutes or until golden. Remove the cooked waffle, keep warm and repeat with the remaining batter.

Serve warm with whipped cream and Spiced Plum Compote.

Bostocks are a new addition to the breakfast repertoire. They are a French concoction I discovered when researching food waste (they were created to use up stale brioche). They are also very decadent and not for the faint-hearted, although you can tone the overall sugar hit down slightly by using stale bread or sourdough, if you prefer. Traditionally, they include orange blossom water, but I am a big fan of apple with almonds, so have altered things somewhat. Make a triple batch of the syrup and store it in the fridge for your next bostock blowout. Serve the bostocks warm out of the oven and add some fresh berries and a dollop of yogurt if you like.

APPLE AND ALMOND BOSTOCK

SERVES 4

125g (4½oz) unsalted butter, softened
125g (4½oz) icing sugar, plus extra
    for dusting
100g (3½oz) ground almonds
½ teaspoon almond extract
1 teaspoon vanilla bean paste
1 egg
50g (1¾oz) plain flour
6–8 pieces of stale brioche or bread
200g (7oz) flaked almonds

For the syrup
150ml (¼ pint) apple juice
150g (5½oz) caster sugar
1 teaspoon vanilla bean paste

Preheat the oven to 200°C (400°F), Gas Mark 6.

First make the syrup. In a saucepan, bring the apple juice, sugar and vanilla to the boil. Cook over a high heat for no more than 1 minute until the sugar has dissolved and you have a light, clear syrup. Set aside.

In a bowl, beat the butter and icing sugar together until light and fluffy. Add the ground almonds, almond extract, vanilla, egg and flour and beat again until the mixture is smooth.

To assemble the bostocks, take a piece of brioche and soak each side in the syrup. Place it on a baking tray and repeat with the remaining slices. Divide the almond batter between the brioche slices and spread it across the top of each slice. Sprinkle generously with the flaked almonds.

Bake for 10–12 minutes or until golden brown and the almond topping is cooked through. Dust with icing sugar and serve warm.

I won't lie – I do enjoy making a croissant from scratch. It is very therapeutic: the folding, laminating, turning… It is, however, exceptionally time-consuming, so is best reserved for days when I am in a particularly cheery mood and prepared to put in the hours. This recipe, on the other hand, is the opposite and is perfect for pleasing overnight guests when you are feeling somewhat fragile and want to use shop-bought croissants. It is very simple to knock up, preferably in your pyjamas, and I find it always receives instant gratification.

HAZELNUT CROISSANTS

MAKES 8

275g (9¾oz) blanched hazelnuts, toasted
100g (3½oz) unsalted butter
100g (3½oz) caster sugar
1 teaspoon vanilla bean paste
8 croissants (a day or so old is fine)
4 tablespoons apricot jam
2 tablespoons water

Preheat the oven to 180°C (350°F), Gas Mark 4.

In a food processor, blitz 200g (7oz) of the toasted hazelnuts for 4–5 minutes. They should become very fine and paste-like. Add the butter, sugar and vanilla and blitz again until smooth.

Cut the croissants in half horizontally and spread a generous amount of the hazelnut paste inside. Place the lids back on top and arrange the filled croissants on a baking tray. Bake for 5–7 minutes, keeping an eye on them so that they don't burn.

While the croissants are cooking, heat the jam with the 2 tablespoons of water in a small saucepan over a medium-high heat. Bring to the boil, then take the pan off the heat but keep the melted jam warm.

Chop the remaining toasted hazelnuts.

When the croissants are ready, brush the tops with the hot jam and sprinkle with the chopped hazelnuts. Serve warm.

If you have ever been in my house between the hours of 10am and 1pm over the weekend, you will almost certainly have been fed these. They were the first thing I made independently and the first recipe I learnt off by heart (I still make them in pounds and ounces). I used them to impress new friends aged 12, for an unsuccessful business venture aged 15, and then they were often produced to show off to hungry hungover boys in the aftermath of a party. They are the most reliable of creations and a lazy morning treat I will never tire of. Serve them with a very large pot of steaming coffee.

DROP SCONES WITH BANANA AND WHIPPED MAPLE BUTTER

MAKES 12

For the drop scones
225g (8oz) self-raising flour
50g (1¾oz) caster sugar
2 eggs
150ml (¼ pint) milk
butter, for greasing

For the whipped maple butter
150g (5½oz) unsalted butter, softened
1 tablespoon golden syrup
50ml (2fl oz) maple syrup
1 teaspoon ground cinnamon
2 tablespoons icing sugar

To serve
chopped bananas
maple syrup
crushed pecan nuts

First make the maple butter. Whip all the ingredients together in a stand mixer until pale, smooth and easily spreadable.

For the drop scones, put the ingredients into a bowl and beat together by hand or using an electric whisk. The mixture should be completely smooth and fairly thick.

Brush a nonstick frying pan with a little butter and heat it over a medium heat. You'll need to cook the drop scones in batches. Using a dessert spoon, spoon dollops of the batter into the pan, spreading them out just a little with the back of the spoon. Cook for about 2 minutes until the surface becomes very bubbly, then flip the drop scones and cook the other sides for a further 1–2 minutes until golden. Stack the cooked drop scones on a clean tea towel and wrap them up to keep them warm, then repeat this process with the remaining batter.

Serve the whipped maple butter in a bowl and allow people to stack up their pancakes with it. Serve with the chopped banana, some more maple syrup and a good scattering of crushed pecan nuts.

This is a breakfast for early autumn mornings when the leaves are beginning to turn and the fruits start to soften. The cherries can, of course, be replaced with other stoned fruits, plums and greengages being excellent alternatives.

CRÊPES WITH ROASTED CHERRIES

SERVES 4

For the crêpes
2 eggs
250g (9oz) plain flour
500ml (18fl oz) milk
sunflower oil

For the roasted cherries
200g (7oz) cherries (Rainier variety, if you can get them), halved and stoned
2 tablespoons clear honey
2 tablespoons brandy (optional)
1 teaspoon vanilla bean paste
knob of butter

To serve
lemon, for squeezing
caster sugar

For the crêpes, whisk the eggs, flour and milk together until smooth. You can use a food processor or a stick blender for this if you would like. Rest the batter in the refrigerator for at least 15 minutes (you can keep it in there overnight if you wish).

Preheat the oven to 200°C (400°F), Gas Mark 6.

Arrange the halved cherries on a roasting tray with the cut sides facing up. Drizzle with the honey, brandy (if using) and vanilla bean paste, then dot small flecks of the butter around the dish. Roast for 10–15 minutes or until the fruit begins to colour a little.

Meanwhile, heat a shallow nonstick frying pan over a medium heat. Use a piece of kitchen paper to wipe a little oil across the surface of the pan. Pour a small ladleful of batter into the pan and swill it around so that it coats the entire base of the pan. Cook for about 2 minutes until the mixture starts to set and bubbles appear, then flip, using a fish slice or palette knife to help you loosen the crêpe. Cook for a further 1–2 minutes on the other side until pale golden, then fold the crêpe into a quarter and set aside – put it on a plate, covered with a clean tea towel, to help keep it warm while you make the others. Repeat the process with the remaining batter.

Serve the crêpes with the roasted cherries, a small squeeze of lemon juice and a sprinkling of caster sugar. (Alternatively, crème fraîche makes a very nice accompaniment.)

I toyed with the name for this recipe a lot. It can arguably be eaten at any time of the day, but as I failed to include a full English (or Scottish!) breakfast in this book, I thought these wee spicy chorizo toasts could be a sort of Spanish equivalent. I love to use a variety of tomatoes, from little round golden ones to plum-shaped Chocolate Cherry – the sweetness varies wildly. You can get a good range of tomatoes in most supermarkets nowadays, but plain little red ones are not to be sniffed at if you can't find any others. If you have any extra tomato-and-chorizo mixture, stir it through a bowl of spaghetti with a good glug of olive oil and enjoy it with a glass of red for the ultimate in comfort food.

BREAKFAST BRUSCHETTA

SERVES 4

200g (7oz) chorizo, finely sliced
450g (1lb) mixed cherry tomatoes, halved
2 garlic cloves, finely sliced
small bunch of fresh oregano, leaves picked
8 slices of your preferred bread
olive oil
4 eggs
salt and cracked pink peppercorns

Preheat the oven to 180°C (350°F), Gas Mark 4.

Arrange the chorizo discs in a deep roasting tray. Cook for 5–10 minutes or until just beginning to colour and a lot of the red oil has escaped. Drain the excess oil and return the meat to the tray.

Chuck the tomatoes into the tray and sprinkle the garlic and oregano leaves over the tomatoes (reserve a few leaves for using later). Season with a little salt. Return the tray to the oven and bake for 10–15 minutes or until the tomatoes have softened and caramelized.

Meanwhile, prepare the bread. Place a griddle pan over a very high heat. Brush each side of the bread with a little olive oil, then toast the bread on the griddle pan. It will only take a few moments on each side – you are looking for charred marks. Set aside, keeping the toasted bread warm.

Once the tomatoes are ready, fry your eggs in some olive oil. I like them to have a crispy bottom and runny yolk, but do them however you and your guests prefer.

Spoon the tomatoes and chorizo on to each slice of bread before topping with an egg. A crack of pink peppercorns and a sprinkling of the reserved oregano leaves will finish the whole thing off.

Known as ca phe sua da *(the literal translation of which is coffee, sweetened milk, ice), this drink is served on the streets of Vietnam, where you can witness glorious showmanship in its creation that captures the attention of passers-by. I would like to make it very clear that this is not a traditional recipe. Having attempted various versions of this little drink without the aid of the specialized Vietnamese coffee filter – or a Vietnamese barista, for that matter – I found this to be the closest to the authentic version and it is simple to make at home. I have taken a bit of creative liberty with the sweetened milk (or condensed milk). As someone that cannot stand sugar in their drinks, I found it all a bit too much and so have opted for dates and agave nectar – both more complex sweeteners that suit coffee's oomph far better than sugar, in my opinion. If you are in need of some indulgence, I would encourage a wee splash of double cream. However, full-fat milk or almond milk work just as well when you need that caffeine hit.*

VIETNAMESE ICED COFFEE

SERVES 4

4 tablespoons ground coffee
200ml (⅓ pint) boiling water
50g (1¾oz) pitted dates
50ml (2fl oz) agave nectar

To serve
ice cubes
double cream, full-fat milk
  or almond milk

Prepare your coffee in a cafetière using the ground coffee and boiling water. Allow to steep for 2–3 minutes before plunging.

Transfer the hot coffee to a food processor or blender with the dates. Blitz on a high speed setting for 2–3 minutes. You are looking for a smooth liquid. Add the agave and blitz again.

Fill 4 glasses with ice cubes and pour the coffee mixture on top until half full. Top up with double cream if you are feeling extra indulgent, or any milk of your choosing. Serve immediately.

*Every spring I have watched Dad march out to the veg patch and plant all sorts.
His hard work is normally met with moans of "We don't like those types of beans!"
or "Why didn't you grow the blue potatoes instead of the boring ones?". He puts
up with a lot. A few years ago, however, I got my hands on a seed catalogue and
proceeded to spend a small fortune on the most elaborate varieties of carrots,
radishes, peas, courgettes, gourds and leaves going. Needless to say, it wasn't the
most successful planting year in terms of produce. An unsheltered Scottish climate
does not provide the perfect conditions for candy beetroot, it would seem. The most
(only) successful veg I chose that year was rainbow chard, a hardy and reliable plant
that can tolerate our atrocious summers. I love chard for the meatiness it brings to
a dish and it is wonderfully versatile, taking on different flavours such as citrus and
spice. It is paired best with fresh herbs, however, and I love this simple and speedy
way of preparing it. If you can't find chard, cavolo nero or curly kale will work well.
This is a great dish for communal eating – simply plonk the pan in the middle of the
table and let people use big hunks of buttered toast to eat it with.*

BAKED EGGS AND SWISS CHARD

SERVES 2–4

150g (5½oz) rainbow chard
olive oil
knob of butter
2 banana shallots, finely sliced
½ teaspoon freshly grated nutmeg
small bunch of fresh marjoram,
    leaves picked (optional)
4 eggs
50g (1¾oz) feta cheese
salt and freshly ground black pepper

To serve
50g (1¾oz) Parmesan cheese, grated

Preheat the oven to 200°C (400°F), Gas Mark 6.

Strip the leaves from the chard stems and set aside. Roughly chop the coloured stems into 2cm (¾ inch) lengths.

Heat a good glug of olive oil and the butter in an ovenproof frying pan. Add the chard stems and sliced shallots and cook over a medium heat for about 5 minutes until softened and beginning to colour. Add the nutmeg and season lightly.

Add the marjoram leaves to the pan along with the chard leaves (you many need to tear those up a little). Stir everything together. Crack the eggs directly on top of the greens, then crumble the feta all over. Transfer the frying pan to the oven and bake for 10 minutes. You want the egg whites to have set but the yolks to remain runny.

Sprinkle the Parmesan over the contents of the frying pan and add some chopped herbs just before serving.

- MENU -

AUTUMNAL BRUNCH

BAKED EGGS AND SWISS CHARD * *see page 42*

BALSAMIC ONION SODA BREAD * *see page 115*

RYE WAFFLES * *see page 31*

SPICED PLUM COMPOTE * *page 262*

STRAWBERRY AND ELDERFLOWER JAM * *see page 258*

CLEMENTINE AND VANILLA MARMALADE * *see page 261*

From left to right: Balsamic onion soda bread;
Baked eggs and Swiss chard; Rye waffles;
Strawberry and elderflower jam; Clementine
and vanilla marmalade; Spiced plum compote.

SMALL PLATES

The almonds in this soup add a creaminess you would normally only achieve using dairy products. It is a lovely light soup that's best knocked up in the springtime for a simple and refreshing lunch.

WATERCRESS AND ALMOND SOUP

SERVES 4–6

olive oil

1 large white onion or 2 banana
  shallots, finely sliced

1 large potato, peeled and grated

75g (2¾oz) ground almonds

2 garlic cloves, finely sliced or minced

1.2 litres (2 pints) vegetable stock

100g (3½oz) broad beans, skinned
  or peas (I buy frozen broad beans
  as they are easier to prep – cover
  with boiling water, allow to sit for
  a minute, then squeeze between
  thumb and forefinger to remove
  the bean)

150g (5½oz) watercress

small bunch of flat leaf parsley,
  leaves picked

salt and freshly ground black pepper

garlic flowers, to garnish (optional)

Heat a splash of oil in a deep saucepan over a medium heat, then add the onion and potato. Sweat the vegetables for about 5 minutes until they begin to become translucent.

Add the almonds, garlic and two-thirds of the vegetable stock to the pan. Bring the liquid to the boil, then cover the pan with a lid, reduce the heat to a medium setting and simmer for 20 minutes.

Now add the broad beans, watercress and parsley. Stir, then take the pan off the heat. You don't want to overcook the greens or they will lose their bright colour. Blitz the soup in a food processor or using a stick blender until very smooth. It will still be very thick at this stage, but it is best to blend at this point as it will result in a much smoother soup. Once you are happy with the texture, add the remaining stock or enough to bring the soup to your preferred consistency. Season to taste before scattering with garlic flowers to garnish, if you like.

I once sat down to this soup with a friend at the end of winter. We had a proper gossip over generous bowls of silky, steaming soup and big chunks of seeded bread. It was heavenly. Apple and celeriac are both pretty warming flavours so you want to enjoy this soup on a dim and dreich *(or dreary, if you're English) day like we did. The basil oil is optional, but I think it is particularly good on soups and salads. I would recommend making extra and storing a wee bottle of it in the fridge for seasoning and dressing other dishes, too. Serve the soup with a drizzle of the oil and some good bread. You could also add a drizzle of cream and some toasted seeds.*

APPLE AND CELERIAC SOUP
WITH BASIL OIL

SERVES 4

knob of butter
1 tablespoon olive oil
2 banana shallots, finely chopped
1 garlic clove, finely chopped
1 large celeriac, peeled deeply with a
   knife and cut into 1cm (½ inch) dice
4–5 smallish potatoes or 3 large ones,
   peeled and cut into 1cm (½ inch) dice
1 green apple, peeled, cored and cut
   into 1cm (½ inch) dice
700ml (1¼ pints) vegetable or chicken
   stock
up to 150ml (¼ pint) apple juice, as
   necessary
salt and freshly ground black pepper

For the basil oil
large handful of basil, leaves picked
65ml (2¼fl oz) olive oil

Heat the butter and oil in a deep saucepan over a medium-low heat. Add the shallots and garlic, put on the pan lid and sweat for about 5 minutes until the shallots begin to soften.

Add the diced celeriac and potatoes to the pan, increase the heat to medium-high and cook for about 5 minutes until the celeriac colours very slightly. Then add the diced apple along with the stock, cover the pan again and cook for 20 minutes until the vegetables are soft. Add a little apple juice if it looks as if a lot of the liquid has evaporated before the vegetables soften.

While the soup is cooking, make the basil oil. Bash the basil leaves using a pestle and mortar or in a bowl with the end of a rolling pin. Once they are paste-like, add the oil bit by bit as you continue to bash the mixture – you should end with a bright green oil. You can either leave it with small flecks of basil leaves or pass the oil through a sieve to filter them out. Either way, the basil oil will keep for about a week if stored in an airtight container in the refrigerator.

After the 20 minutes of cooking time has elapsed, remove the lid from the soup pot and cook for a further 5–10 minutes, again adding apple juice if the mixture seems too thick. Then take the pan off the heat and blitz the mixture with a stick blender until very smooth. Season to taste, then serve the soup with a drizzling of the basil oil on each bowlful.

This is the sort of broth that cures and revives people. Remedying and big on flavour, it is the very embodiment of food for the soul.

CHICKEN AND ORZO BROTH

SERVES 4–6

olive oil
1 leek (pale green and white sections
   only), finely chopped
1 banana shallot, finely chopped
2 large celery sticks, finely chopped
1.2 litres (2 pints) chicken stock
   (see below for homemade, or
   good-quality shop bought)
100g (3½oz) orzo pasta
400g (14oz) leftover roast chicken
   (breast and thigh meat), roughly torn
100g (3½oz) peas (optional)
juice of ½ lemon
salt and freshly ground black pepper
small handful of fresh dill, to garnish

For the homemade stock (optional)
1 leftover cooked chicken carcass,
   meat stripped
any leftover roast vegetables
   (optional)
1 red onion, finely chopped
dark green tip of 1 medium leek (the
   top 5cm/2 inches), finely chopped

If you're making your own stock, preheat the oven to 140°C (275°F), Gas Mark 1.

Place the chicken in a deep casserole dish and add any roast veg you have, the chopped onion and the leek. Cover with cold water. Place the lid on top, transfer to the oven and cook for at least 6 hours, preferably overnight. The following morning, you should have a reduced golden stock, rich with flavour. Strain, cover and set aside in the refrigerator until required.

For the soup, heat a good glug of oil in a deep saucepan and add the leek, shallot and celery. Sweat for 5–10 minutes over a low heat until beginning to turn translucent. Add the stock. Cover the pan with a lid and cook for a further 5–10 minutes to develop the flavours.

Add the orzo and cover again. The pasta will take roughly 8 minutes to cook, so keep an eye on it. A few minutes before the pasta is ready, add the roast chicken and the peas, if using. Take the pan off the heat the minute the pasta is ready. Stir in the lemon juice and season to taste. Scatter with some fronds of dill just before serving.

I love this soup for its luxurious colour and earthy flavour. Who wouldn't be grinning when served a bright fuchsia-coloured bowl of soup?

BORSCHT

SERVES 4–6

olive oil
2 red onions, finely chopped
2 large celery sticks, finely chopped
1 large carrot (purple, if you can get it), finely chopped
750g (1lb 10oz) raw beetroot, peeled and finely chopped
1 litre (1¾ pints) vegetable stock
2 garlic cloves, finely sliced or minced
5 tablespoons vodka (optional)

To serve
55g (2oz) feta cheese
fresh dill fronds

Heat a good glug of olive oil in a deep saucepan and add the onions, celery and carrot. Cook over a medium heat for 5–10 minutes until the vegetables begin to soften and colour ever so slightly.

Add the beetroot to the pan and cook for a further 5–10 minutes. Now add the stock and garlic. Cover and allow to simmer for around 30 minutes. To test if the beetroot is cooked, use the back of a teaspoon to squash a piece of it. It should be soft all the way through.

Add the vodka, if using, and continue to cook for 5 minutes to allow the alcohol to burn off. Take the pan off the heat and leave the soup to stand for 5 minutes, then blitz the soup in a food processor or using a stick blender – you want the texture to be very smooth. Serve with a crumbling of feta and a few fronds of fresh dill.

I remember mum sprouting sprouts during the summer holidays. For what felt like days and days there would be a jar half filled with water and beans, with a funny mesh on top to let air in and drain the water once it became murky. This sight used to terrify me, as it meant that very soon Mum would sabotage perfectly nice leaves with these sour pulses with tails. I detested them. Now that I'm slightly older and only a little wiser, I love them for their texture and bitter, earthy flavours. They are also very cheap to produce and require nothing but some water, sunshine and a little love – just like us all, really.

SPROUT SALAD
WITH PEANUTS AND SESAME

SERVES 4

¼ large white cabbage, finely
   shredded into long, thin ribbons
handful of flat leaf parsley or rocket,
   finely chopped
250g (9oz) mixed sprouts
150g (5½oz) roasted peanuts

For the seedy dressing
4 tablespoons olive oil
1 teaspoon agave nectar
2 teaspoons lemon juice
1 tablespoon white wine vinegar
30g (1oz) pumpkin seeds, toasted
30g (1oz) pine nuts, toasted
20g (¾oz) black or white sesame seeds
salt and freshly ground black pepper

For the dressing, in a small bowl whisk the oil, agave, lemon juice and vinegar together. Season lightly.

Put all the salad ingredients into a large bowl.

Add the toasted pumpkin seeds and pine nuts to the dressing along with the sesame seeds.

Toss the salad with the seedy dressing and allow the dressed salad to sit for 5 minutes before serving.

This is a big, colourful splatter of a dish, the sort of plate you could take to the table and everyone will instantly smile. It has the same crunch and texture as a good coleslaw, and is best paired with white fish, such as sea bass, and maybe a salsa verde for a light summer supper. You can, of course, use regular beetroots for this salad, but they will bleed into the other colours.

BEETROOT AND RADISH SALAD

SERVES 4–6

3 candy (or Chioggia) beetroots
3 golden beetroots
3 carrots
7–10 radishes
handful of pink baby salad leaves
(such as radicchio or red chicory)

For the dressing
juice of ½ lemon
1 tablespoon red wine vinegar
3 tablespoons olive oil
salt and cracked pink peppercorns

Peel and wash your beetroots and carrots. Using a mandoline or your exceptional knife skills and a very sharp knife, very finely slice them along with the radishes, then place in a large bowl.

In a separate bowl, whisk the lemon juice, vinegar and oil together. Season with a little salt.

Toss the dressing through the vegetables and transfer the mixture to a big serving dish. Scatter over the salad leaves and crack some pink peppercorns over the top to serve.

A potato salad, but not as you know it. Nae mayo. Nae chives. And it's served warm. This is delicious and satisfying on a winter's night with a big roast and plenty of company. The kick of chilli will keep you cosy, too!

THE NEW POTATO SALAD

SERVES 4–6

750g (1lb 10oz) new potatoes
3–4 red onions
olive oil
2 teaspoons dried chilli flakes
1 x 400g (14oz) can butter beans, drained
salt and freshly ground black pepper

Bring the potatoes to the boil in a large pan of salted water. Boil for 15–20 minutes, depending on their size, or until they are just underdone. Drain and allow to cool for a moment.

Preheat the oven to 200°C (400°F), Gas Mark 6.

Slice your onions horizontally so that you have full rings with a thickness of approximately 1–2cm (½–¾ inch). Push out the central rings to separate the rings of onion.

Slice the now-cooled potatoes into discs, also about 1–2cm (½–¾ inch) thick. Lay the potato slices out in a large roasting tray alongside the onion slices. Drizzle with some oil and use your hands to mix and coat everything in the oil. Sprinkle with the chilli flakes and butter beans and mix once more. Season lightly, then roast for 20–25 minutes. The potatoes should be golden and the onion, beginning to caramelize.

Toasted sandwiches and wraps are a bit of a thing in our house. We take great delight in layering up grand sandwiches of any flavour, to be charred on the outside and oozy on the inside. This one is my favourites, and can be improved on only with a dollop of Poor Man's Pesto (see page 69).

MUSHROOM AND BRIE SARNIES

SERVES 2–4

olive oil

knob of butter

400g (14oz) mushrooms, cut into
  5mm (¼ inch) slices

small bunch of flat leaf parsley, leaves
  picked and chopped

8 slices of sourdough bread

1 garlic clove, halved

200g (7oz) Brie, sliced

100g (3½oz) spinach, plus extra
  to serve

salt and freshly ground black pepper

Heat a little oil and the butter in a large frying pan over a medium heat. Once hot, add the mushrooms and a little seasoning and fry for 2–3 minutes or until the mushrooms begin to soften. Toss the chopped parsley through them, then transfer the mushrooms to a bowl.

Place the bread slices in the same frying pan, a few slices at a time (depending on the size of your frying pan), and toast on one side. Rub a cut side of the garlic clove over the toasted side of each bit of bread.

To assemble the sandwiches, place a few slices of Brie on top of the toasted side of one piece of bread. Top with a quarter of the mushrooms and a small handful of spinach. Place a second piece of bread on top, this time, with the toasted side facing down. Repeat the process with the remaining ingredients to assemble the rest of the toasties.

Add a little more oil to the pan along with whatever is left of the garlic clove. Carefully transfer the sandwiches to the pan. Place a plate or heavy board on top of all the sandwiches and cook for 2–3 minutes or until browned. Flip the sandwiches carefully to toast the final side and, again, place the plate or board on top. Serve hot with a little more spinach.

For as long as I can remember, a huge fennel plant has grown at the top of the vegetable patch, and for many years my sister Hebe and I avoided it like the plague. It had a funny texture with "feathery" bits that Mum sneaked into salads – I still recall the sense of betrayal when picking through salad leaves to find them. It also had a strange flavour we couldn't identify but reminded us ever so slightly of toothpaste. So, yes, fennel didn't have a lot going for it when I was wee. Recently, however, I have started to use fennel in many dishes, both sweet and savoury, in fresh and seed form, and fennel and I have finally made our peace – its green fronds have since found their way into every salad I have made this year.

SUNSHINE SALAD (COURGETTE, MANGETOUT, FENNEL, CORIANDER)

SERVES 4–6

2 large fennel bulbs
2 small courgettes, preferably
    1 green and 1 yellow
150g (5½oz) mangetout
small bunch of fresh coriander
    (about 30g/1oz), leaves picked

For the dressing
juice of ½ orange
juice of ½ lemon
3 tablespoons olive oil, plus extra
    to serve
1 tablespoon white wine vinegar
salt and freshly ground black pepper

First make the dressing. Whisk the citrus juices, oil and vinegar together in a bowl. Season to taste.

Using a mandoline or good knife skills and a very sharp knife, finely slice the fennel and reserve the feathery fronds. Add the slices to the dressing in the bowl and toss through to stop the fennel from browning. At this stage you can cover the bowl with clingfilm and store the fennel in the refrigerator for up to 6 hours.

Finely slice the courgettes into ribbons using a vegetable peeler or mandoline. Add the ribbons to the bowl with the fennel and stir through to coat the courgette slices with the dressing.

Finely slice the mangetout (preferably on the diagonal) and mix through the salad.

Pick off the coriander leaves and use to finish the salad with a few of the fennel fronds.

Drizzle extra olive oil on top to finish if you like.

I read once that when radicchio first became widely available, chefs, particularly in America, bought it by the ton and served huge crimson salads made solely with these bitter leaves. It was a fad that promptly came to a stop, as the taste of the salads was so strong that diners refused to eat them. A few decades on, all forms of chicory and endive are very much back in fashion. I find that finely slicing any type of endive and dressing it well helps to combat the bitterness, and enhances some of the nutty tones present in the leaf. You can also grill the leaves to release the warmer flavours, but I am yet to embrace the cooking-your-leaves trend – it just feels wrong! I love serving this salad towards the end of winter when the flavour of the leaves is at its best and you no longer crave big hearty bowls of hot food. Add some good Serrano ham and a few boiled potatoes for a more robust meal.

RADICCHIO, FIG AND APPLE SALAD
WITH WALNUT DRESSING

SERVES 4–6

2 red dessert apples
good splash of apple juice
1 large head of radicchio, cut into
    rough strips
8 small figs, cut or torn into quarters
100g (3½oz) Chaource cheese (or
    any creamy cows' or goats' cheese),
    crumbled or sliced
baby salad leaves

For the dressing
75g (2¾oz) walnuts, toasted
2 tablespoons clear honey
100ml (3½fl oz) light olive oil
1 tablespoon red wine vinegar
salt and freshly ground black pepper

First make the dressing. Put the toasted walnuts, honey and half the oil into a food processor and blitz on a high speed until the mixture is fairly smooth. Add the remaining oil and the vinegar and blitz again. Season the dressing with salt and pepper to taste.

Prepare the apples soon before you put the salad together, to prevent them from oxidizing and going brown. Core the apples, then slice them finely. Put them into a large bowl and cover with the apple juice, which helps to prevent oxidation.

Just before serving, toss the apples, radicchio and figs together with some of the walnut dressing in the bowl. Transfer the mixture to a shallow serving plate and finish with the cheese and baby salad leaves. Drizzle over the remaining dressing to serve.

There is a great French restaurant in Perth called Pig'Halle. Growing up, we very rarely ate out, so when we did it was always a treat and we almost always went to Pig'Halle. Every meal began with their fantastic bread served with a wee dish of their unbelievably delicious rillettes. My sister Hebe and myself would battle over the little ceramic pot, scraping out every last morsel. Below is my homage to that delicious dish. Serve it with thick slabs of toast and some pickles.

PORK RILLETTES

SERVES 4–6

approximately 500g (1lb 2oz) pork belly
2 sprigs of rosemary
2 sprigs of thyme
2 bay leaves
10 black peppercorns
½ garlic bulb
1 teaspoon grainy mustard
175ml (6fl oz) boiling water

Preheat the oven to 140°C (275°F), Gas Mark 1.

Place all the ingredients in a deep roasting tray or ovenproof dish and cook for at least 3 hours.

Once the meat is falling apart, remove it from the tray or dish – leaving behind, but reserving, any liquid – and shred it roughly using 2 forks. Place the meat in a food processor and blitz for a moment or so until the meat has been broken down but still has a little texture.

Strain the cooking liquid to remove the herbs, peppercorns and garlic, then pour it into the food processor over the meat. Pulse only for a moment, then divide the mixture between 4 or 6 deep ramekins or pots. Refrigerate overnight to allow the liquid to set.

Pesto is one of those rare things that is far cheaper to buy at the shops than it is to make. It is also universally adored – I have yet to meet anyone over the age of two that isn't a fan. This recipe is one you can adapt and change to suit what greens, seeds and nuts you have to hand, the cheaper the better. It is delicious tossed through boiled new potatoes and served with boiled eggs and some watercress. And it keeps well in the fridge – an easy, breezy summer recipe for all. If you are making it for someone with a nut allergy, simply replace the almonds/pistachios with more seeds.

POOR MAN'S PESTO

SERVES 4–6

50g (1¾oz) mixed nuts (almonds or
  pistachios are best; for a not-so-
  poor man's pesto, use pine nuts)
50g (1¾oz) mixed seeds (I love a
  mixture of pumpkin, sunflower and
  sesame seeds)
150–200g (5½–7oz) mixed green
  leaves (a mixture of spinach, rocket,
  watercress, basil, mint and flat leaf
  parsley works well), roughly torn
100ml (3½fl oz) olive oil, plus extra
  as needed
juice of ½ lemon
2 garlic cloves, finely chopped
  or minced
20g (¾oz) Manchego cheese,
  finely grated
salt and freshly ground black pepper

Set a frying pan over a medium heat and lightly toast your nuts and seeds for 8 minutes or until they are fragrant and have turned a light golden colour. Transfer them to a dish and leave to cool.

Put the torn leaves into a food processor, then add the cooled toasted nuts and seeds, the oil, lemon juice and garlic. Blitz on a high speed setting until the mixture is fairly smooth in texture.

Transfer the mixture to a bowl and stir in the grated cheese. Season to taste. If you want the pesto to have a looser consistency, add a little more oil. Transfer the mixture to a sterilized jar, cover with a layer of oil and seal. Store in the refrigerator for up to 1 week.

This might be the dish in this book that I crave the most. A big plate of greens instantly makes me feel brighter. The quinoa adds nuttiness and some bulk to the dish, and I would urge you to use the black onion seeds if you can source them. Slightly bitter and almost salty in taste, they help to season the salad and provide a lovely visual pop against the green. Perfect for a Monday night dinner served with leftover roast chicken.

GREENS, QUINOA AND BLACK ONION SEED SALAD

SERVES 4–6

150g (5½oz) quinoa
100g (3½oz) green beans, trimmed
  and roughly chopped
100g (3½oz) fine asparagus, woody
  ends snapped off, roughly chopped
100g (3½oz) Tenderstem broccoli,
  trimmed, cut into florets
100g (3½oz) podded broad beans
2 avocados
4 spring onions
olive oil, for drizzling
freshly ground black pepper

For the dressing
juice of 1 lemon
3 tablespoons olive oil
1 tablespoon white wine vinegar
1 teaspoon Dijon mustard
3 tablespoons black onion seeds
salt and freshly ground black pepper

Cook the quinoa following the packet instructions.

Meanwhile, half-fill a separate saucepan with water and bring to the boil. Cook the green beans, asparagus, broccoli and broad beans in batches, letting them cook in the water for no longer than 1–1½ minutes. Drain and allow to cool. Skin your broad beans.

To make the dressing, whisk the lemon juice, oil, vinegar and mustard together. Once the mixture is smooth, stir in the black onion seeds. Season to taste and pour into a serving dish.

Halve, stone and finely slice the avocado and finely slice the spring onions. Toss through the dressing. Add the skinned broad beans and now-cooled greens and mix again.

Drain the quinoa when it is cooked and add a little drizzle of oil and some pepper. Mix well, then stir into the salad. Serve immediately.

Hummus is a lot more than blitzed watery chickpeas. You can use almost any peas, beans or vegetables to create something vibrant and tangy that's great on toasts, crisps and so on. This particular version is perfect for crudités, especially crunchy radishes with the peppery greens still attached. You could also omit the tahini or peanut butter and create a very creamy affair by adding some artichokes or butter beans instead.

WHITE BEAN AND TAHINI HUMMUS

SERVES 4–6

240g (8½oz) cannellini beans
   (drained weight – use roughly
   1 x 400g/14oz can)
50g (1¾oz) tahini or peanut butter
juice of ½ large lemon
1 large garlic clove
2 tablespoons olive oil, plus extra
   for drizzling
salt and freshly ground black pepper
fresh herbs, to garnish (optional)
Fast Flatbreads, to serve (see page 76)

Place all the ingredients in a food processor and blitz until smooth. If the mixture is too thick, add a little more oil or lemon juice. Season a little, then blend again. Taste the mixture to ensure you have got the balance right with the seasoning. (For an extra citrus kick, add the zest of the lemon, too.

Garnish with an extra drizzle of oil and fresh herbs, then serve with Fast Flatbreads, if you like.

I love to eat this smoky, citrusy and deliciously creamy pâté for lunch,
piled high on slabs of good toast and, if possible, outside in the sunshine.

MACKEREL PÂTÉ

SERVES 4–6

300g (10½oz) smoked mackerel fillets
75g (2¾oz) good-quality mayonnaise
juice of 1 lime
freshly ground black pepper

To serve
toast
cress
lemon wedges

Remove the skin from the mackerel and break up the flesh into a food processor. I tend to break the fish in half and run my finger down the spine to check for any bones. Add the mayo and lime juice, then season with pepper. Whizz until you have a smooth pâté. (You can also mash the mixture with a fork, as my mum has done for years. The result is equally delicious but the texture will be a little coarser.)

Serve with toast, cress and lemon wedges for squeezing over.

These go perfectly with the White Bean and Tahini Hummus on page 72 and the Mackerel Paté on page 75, but are also great to make for lunch in a hurry. I have even made pizzas with them before – simply prepare the flatbreads as instructed below, then top with passata, black pepper and mozzarella and cook in a hot oven for 5–10 minutes.

FAST FLATBREADS

MAKES 8

100g (3½oz) natural yogurt
50ml (2fl oz) milk
pinch of salt
½ teaspoon baking powder
250g (9oz) plain flour

Mix all the ingredients together in a bowl until you have a rough dough. Knead the dough for a few minutes until smooth – it does not need to be elastic like a standard bread dough.

Divide the dough into 8 equal portions and roll out each lump using a rolling pin until it has a thickness of 5mm (¼ inch). While you are doing this, heat a frying pan or griddle pan over a high heat until screaming hot.

Cook the rolled-out pieces of dough in batches if necessary. Place them in the pan and cook for 2 minutes, then turn them over and cook for a further 1–2 minutes – the flatbreads should be blistered with slight charring and puff up noticeably. Enjoy hot or cold.

There is a great Scandi bakery based in Edinburgh called Peter's Yard. They make the best crispbreads I have ever tasted and, thankfully, now sell packets of them to good farm shops and delis. If you are lucky enough to see them, snap them up quickly and enjoy selfishly. Failing that, this recipe is the next best thing and took a lot of tweaking to get even close to the Peter's Yard originals. These crispbreads are fantastic served with a dolly mixture of dips, cheese and meats.

HONEY CRISPBREADS

❋

MAKES APPROXIMATELY 18

100g (3½oz) rye flour
100g (3½oz) wholemeal spelt flour, plus extra for dusting
2 tablespoons olive oil, plus extra for greasing
1 tablespoon clear honey
7g sachet (2 teaspoons) fast-action dried yeast
5 tablespoons water
100g (3½oz) mixed seeds (I use a mixture of sesame, fennel, poppy, pumpkin and sunflower seeds)
salt and freshly ground black pepper

In a bowl, mix all the ingredients bar the mixed seeds together and knead on an oiled work surface for 5 minutes. The dough doesn't need to be as elastic as a normal bread dough, but it does require a bit of working. Resist the temptation to add any more flour – the oiled work surface should be enough to prevent too much sticking. Place the dough in an oiled bowl and cover with clingfilm. Leave to rest for 45–60 minutes.

Preheat the oven to 180°C (350°F), Gas Mark 4 towards the end of the resting time.

Once the dough has rested, tip it out on to your work surface and knock it back. Divide it equally into 2 and roll out each portion into a long rectangle about 10cm (4 inches) wide. You want the dough to be as thin as possible, so use a little flour to prevent tearing. If you are lucky enough to own a pasta maker, you can use this to roll out the dough. (Roll it through the stages, starting from the thickest, as you would if making pasta. The result will be a very fine cracker.)

Once the dough is thin enough, use a sharp knife to cut it into strips about 3–4cm (1¼–1½ inches) wide. Transfer these to a baking tray. Brush each cracker with a little water, then sprinkle the seeds on top. Bake for 9–12 minutes or until golden and crisp throughout. Store in an airtight container for up to 1 month.

- MENU -
SPRING LADIES LUNCH

BLOOD ORANGE VODKA BLUSH * *see page 202*

BEEF WITH QUINOA, LENTILS, RADISHES
AND A PARSLEY DRESSING * *see page 172*

SUNSHINE SALAD * *see page 62*

WHITE BEAN AND TAHINI HUMMUS * *see page 72*

FAST FLATBREADS * *see page 76*

ASPARAGUS AND RICOTTA TART * *see page 116*

FIGS AND POMEGRANATES WITH CLOTTED CREAM * *see page 279*

On the table: Blood orange vodka blush;
Beef with quinoa, lentils, radishes and a parsley
dressing; White bean and tahini hummus;
Fast flatbreads.

FOOD TO FLING
TOGETHER

This is a recipe for Ally, Seb, Will, James, Jack and Jed. I have known Ally since I was three, and at one of his parties, I promised a recipe to him and his flatmates out of a generosity somewhat inspired by my slight intoxication. I don't like to break promises and, as it is almost a curry, it seemed fitting for six boys that like their spice. Glasgow Street lads, this one is for you.

THAI GREEN SOUP

SERVES 4–6

125g (4½oz) rice noodles
1 tablespoon olive oil
600ml (20fl oz) vegetable stock
400ml (14fl oz) coconut milk
8–12 raw tiger or king prawns, peeled
lemon and lime juice, to taste
125g (4½oz) mangetout, diagonally
  sliced
75g (2¾oz) spinach
salt and freshly ground black pepper

For the curry paste
5cm (2 inch) fresh root ginger, peeled
  and roughly chopped
3 garlic cloves, roughly chopped
1 lemon grass stick, bashed
small bunch of fresh coriander,
  leaves and stems roughly torn
½ teaspoon ground coriander
1 banana shallot, roughly sliced
1 green chilli, deseeded and
  roughly sliced
2 fresh kaffir lime leaves
finely grated zest of 1 lemon
finely grated zest of 1 lime
2 tablespoons fish sauce

To garnish
4–5 spring onions, sliced
small bunch of Thai basil or fresh
  coriander, leaves picked and chopped
1 green chilli, sliced
lime wedges

First make the curry paste. Put all the paste ingredients into a food processor and blitz on a high speed until you have a smooth paste.

Cook the rice noodles following the packet instructions, then drain and set aside.

Heat the oil in a large saucepan set over a high heat. Add the paste and cook for 3–4 minutes. Pour in the vegetable stock and coconut milk and bring to the boil. Add the prawns, reduce the heat to low and simmer for about 10 minutes until the prawns turn a lovely pink. Season the soup to taste using salt, pepper and the juice from the lemon and lime that were zested for the paste (you may not require all the juice).

Put the garnishes in wee bowls for people to help themselves. Divide the drained noodles between 4 or 6 bowls.

When ready to serve, stir the mangetout and spinach into the soup, then take the pan off the heat immediately. Ladle the soup over the noodles and serve with the garnishes alongside.

This is the most simple and, arguably, most delicious way to cook fish. The trout stays moist and the flesh becomes a beautiful shade of pink. I think there is a lot to be said for serving fish whole, not just for simplicity but also for flavour. I love this dish for summer eating, and don't see anything wrong with serving your guests the whole bag. Much like a present, the fun is in the unwrapping! This dish is best served in the spring or summer with boiled new potatoes and a hearty load of greens. The Sunshine Salad (see page 62) is a particular favourite of mine and an ideal accompaniment for the trout.

PAPER BAG TROUT

SERVES 4

2 large (or 4 small) rainbow trout
1 lemon, finely sliced
1 lime, finely sliced
2 spring onions, halved lengthways
small bunch of fresh dill
small bunch of fresh parsley
4 radishes, finely sliced
olive oil
salt and freshly ground black pepper

Preheat the oven to 200°C (400°F), Gas Mark 6.

You can ask your fishmonger to prepare your fish for you, but if you are using fish you've caught yourself, you'll need to gut them and remove the gills. To do this, make a large cut along the belly of each fish, from tail end to throat, taking care not to cut into the internal organs. Using your hands, carefully scrape out the internal organs, ensuring you don't break them open. Open up the gills and cut away the frilled sections – these will make the fish taste unpleasant if left in. Rinse the gutted fish carefully and thoroughly to remove all traces of the entrails.

Grab a large rectangle of greaseproof paper and place a fish (or 2 wee ones) on one half of the rectangle. Arrange a few slices of lemon and lime inside the cavity of the fish, then place a few slices on top. Put 2 spring onion halves, a sprig of dill and a sprig of parsley on top of the fish. Scatter over some radish slices, then tie your herb bunch and citrus in place using a piece of string. Drizzle with olive oil and season lightly. Fold the remaining half of the greaseproof paper over the prepared fish, then fold all the corresponding edges of the paper over themselves multiple times to completely seal the fish. Repeat with the remaining fish, vegetables and citrus fruit slices using another rectangle of greaseproof paper. Place the parcels on a baking tray and bake for 18–20 minutes, depending on the size of your fish.

If you've used 4 small trout, you could serve each person a bag individually and leave them to open it up themselves. If you've used 2 large trout, place both bags on a large serving plate and encourage your diners to dig in.

As a Scot, I am probably hardwired to like pearl barley – think of Scotch broth, to give you an idea of how much this grain is in the blood for Scots. But what I love doing with pearl barley most of all is using it for risottos. The flavour and texture becomes more wholesome when cooked in this way, I reckon. This flavour matches perfectly with earthy wild mushrooms. Although the cooking principle is the same as with any risotto, bear in mind that it will take a little longer. Feed, stir and repeat. And I won't apologize for two risotto recipes in one book. I adore risotto and you will thank me later anyway.

PEARL BARLEY AND MUSHROOM RISOTTO

SERVES 4

olive oil

2 banana shallots or 1 large white
  onion, finely chopped

4 garlic cloves, finely chopped

300g (10½oz) pearl barley

1 litre (1¾ pints) hot chicken or
  vegetable stock

300g (10½oz) mixed mushrooms
  (I like to use chestnut mushrooms,
  chanterelles and Asian varieties),
  finely chopped

2–3 sprigs of thyme, leaves picked
  and finely chopped

100ml (3½fl oz) double or extra-thick
  cream

salt and freshly ground black pepper

50g (1¾oz) Parmesan cheese, grated
  to garnish

Heat the oil in a large saucepan over a medium heat. Add the shallots and garlic and cook until the shallots are translucent, sweet and just beginning to colour. Add the pearl barley and cook for a further minute or so to toast the grains.

Add a good splash of the stock and bring to the boil, then reduce to a simmer and allow the stock to be absorbed, stirring constantly. When the stock is nearly all absorbed, add another splash. Repeat the process until the stock is finished or the pearl barley is just about cooked. It should feel soft and swollen.

Add the mushrooms to the pan with the thyme and seasoning. Turn the heat off and stir the risotto for 1–2 minutes. Add the cream and stir well. Serve with a good grating of the cheese.

Tacos are my father's idea of living hell. A messy open tortilla that you have to fill yourself and then eat with your hands. They are the sort of chaos he cannot stand at dinner time. My sisters and I, however, take great pleasure in watching him panic and make a terrible job of the whole thing, and I cook them regularly because of this. These quick versions are perfect for weekday eating and are great when feeding friends.

SPEEDY SPICY TACOS

SERVES 4

2 tablespoons olive oil

1 large red onion or 2 shallots, finely chopped

2 garlic cloves, finely chopped

2 teaspoons smoked paprika

1 teaspoon ground cumin

2 tablespoons tomato purée

6–8 radishes, sliced

3–4 spring onions, sliced

small bunch of fresh coriander, leaves picked and chopped

400g (14oz) minced pork

dried chilli flakes, to taste

8 soft tortillas

2 avocados, peeled, stoned and sliced then lime juice squeezed over

1 lime, cut into wedges

½–1 small fresh chilli, finely sliced diagonally

160g (5¾oz) natural yogurt

chilli sauce, to taste

salt and freshly ground black pepper

Preheat the oven to 170°C (340°F), Gas Mark 3½.

Heat the olive oil in a deep saucepan over a medium heat and add the onion. Cook for a few minutes until it begins to soften, then add the garlic, paprika, cumin and tomato purée. Cover with a lid and allow the onion and garlic to soften and the onion to become translucent.

Meanwhile, you can prepare the radishes, spring onions and coriander, and place them in bowls.

Add the minced pork to the now-translucent onions. Stir to combine, then increase the heat to high and cook for approximately 12 minutes until the meat darkens in colour. If it dries out too much, add a little hot water. Season with chilli flakes, salt and pepper to taste and transfer to a serving bowl.

Wrap the stack of tortillas in kitchen foil and heat in the oven for 8–10 minutes or following the packet instructions – this will soften them up.

Put the sliced avocados, lime wedges and wee slivers of the chilli into bowls. Put the yogurt in a separate bowl and spike with swirls of chilli sauce. Put these bowls on the table along with the bowls of spring onion, radish and coriander for people to help themselves.

Transfer the warmed tortillas to a serving platter, then add this to the table with the bowl of minced pork and get stuck in. Make as much of a mess as my father would!

These wee wraps are vibrant and refreshing, and are great for a lunch spread full of small plates or as a pre-dinner nibble if cut in half. I love the tanginess of the grapefruit with the soft creamy crab and avocado, but if you are not a fan of that marriage, feel free to omit the grapefruit.

RAINBOW RICE PAPER ROLLS

MAKE 16

16 rice paper wrappers

For the filling
selection of edible flowers (such as pansies, garlic flowers and nasturtiums)
400g (14oz) white crab meat
2 avocados, peeled stoned and finely sliced
½ cucumber, deseeded and cut into fine vertical slices
4 spring onions, finely shredded
½ pink grapefruit, peeled, segmented and very finely sliced
small bunch of fresh coriander, leaves picked
1 small head of crispy lettuce, shredded
50g (1¾oz) white sesame seeds

For the dipping sauce
1 tablespoon caster sugar
juice of 1 large lime
1 tablespoon fish sauce
1 garlic clove, minced
2 tablespoons white sesame seeds or crushed roasted peanuts

Fill a large shallow bowl with warm water. Soak a wrapper in the water for a few seconds to soften it a little (it will soften further as you work with it), then lay it on a chopping board or work surface.

Press a few pansies (or whichever flowers you are using) face down in a row across the top half of the wrapper (furthest from you). Stack a dolly mixture of your fillings on the wrapper in a row below the flowers, packing them together as tightly as possible. It doesn't matter about which order the ingredients go into the wrapper, or how much or how little of each ingredient you use – make the rolls to your taste.

Fold the right and left sides of the wrapper inwards over the fillings, then roll up the wrapper from the edge closest to you, keeping the filling ingredients tightly packed together as you roll. Because the flowers are positioned on the last part of the wrapper to be rolled up, they should be clearly visible on the outside of the roll through the final layer of the translucent wrapper. Place the roll on a plate with the seam facing downwards. Repeat with the remaining wrappers and filling. Ensure the finished rolls do not touch one another on the plate, as they will stick. Keep the finished rolls covered with a damp cloth as you are working.

To make the dipping sauce, mix all the ingredients together in a jug until the sugar has dissolved. Serve in a wee bowl on the side of the rolls.

On a very last-minute trip to Edinburgh one foggy Friday night, I made plans to see my aunty for dinner. Of course, we couldn't get a table anywhere. After a bit of frantic searching we ended up agreeing to a 30-minute slot at The Dogs on Hanover Street, before we got turfed out to make way for those who had actually made reservations. We both wolfed down little speckled bowls of asparagus risotto and a brownie with stout ice cream, and necked a glass of white each. Though rushed, it was one of the best risottos I have had and I've tried to recreate it ever since, minus the time frame! This dish is excellent for a weeknight gathering. There is something very satisfying about having a blether with your friends in the kitchen while tending to a risotto with a glass in hand. That is how entertaining should be, I reckon.

ASPARAGUS RISOTTO

SERVES 4

2 tablespoons olive oil, plus extra
  for drizzling
small knob of butter
2 banana shallots, finely chopped
250g (9oz) risotto or Arborio rice
125ml (4fl oz) white wine
2 garlic cloves, minced
700ml (1¼ pints) hot chicken or
  vegetable stock
300g (10½oz) asparagus, woody ends
  snapped off, diagonally sliced into
  1cm (½ inch) lengths
25g (1oz) Parmesan cheese, grated
small bunch of mint, leaves picked
  and finely chopped
salt and freshly ground black pepper

In a large frying pan, heat the oil and butter over a high heat. Add the shallots and rice and fry for 5 minutes until the shallots are cooked and the rice is just beginning to colour. Pour in the wine, add the garlic, reduce the heat to medium and allow to cook for 2–3 minutes.

Now you simply have to feed the risotto a ladleful of stock at a time. Stir in a ladleful, then keep stirring the mixture and only add the next ladleful when the previous one has been almost completely absorbed – it is this process that results in a creamy risotto. When you've added three-quarters of the stock, add the asparagus and stir it through.

Once you've added all the stock (which should take about 25 minutes) and the risotto is cooked, take the pan off the heat. Add the Parmesan and mint and beat the risotto to ensure they are well mixed in. Season to taste, then serve.

This very subtle dish is perfect for midweek suppers when you want something warming but fairly quick to prep. By cooking the couscous in the same pan as the chicken, you can guarantee that no flavour is lost. I adore giant wholewheat couscous for its bite and slightly nutty flavour, but you can of course use the regular stuff if preferred.

SHERRY AND TARRAGON CHICKEN
WITH PEARL COUSCOUS

SERVES 4

4 large chicken breasts, halved on
   the diagonal
olive oil
2 banana shallots, cut into eighths
5 tablespoons sherry
5 tablespoons dry white wine
small bunch of tarragon,
   leaves picked
300ml (½ pint) chicken stock
200g (7oz) giant couscous
salt and freshly ground black pepper

To garnish
½ small bunch of fresh flat leaf
   parsley, leaves picked
50g (1¾oz) pine nuts, toasted

Preheat the oven to 200°C (400°F), Gas Mark 6.

Season the halved chicken breasts with a little pepper. Heat a good glug of olive oil in a large frying pan, then add the chicken pieces and cook over a medium heat for 2 minutes or so until the undersides are light golden in colour. Turn over the chicken pieces and cook for a further 2–3 minutes. Transfer the chicken to a deep ovenproof dish and set aside.

Reduce the heat under the frying pan to medium-low, then add the shallots and cook for just a few minutes until lightly coloured. Spoon the shallots over the chicken in the ovenproof dish.

Add the sherry, white wine and tarragon to the frying pan, then increase the heat to high and boil for 2–3 minutes to allow the liquids to reduce a little. Add the stock and continue to boil for a few minutes.

Pour one-third of the sauce on top of the chicken in the ovenproof dish or enough so that both the meat and the shallots are submerged in the golden liquid. Transfer the dish to the oven and cook for 15–20 minutes or until the chicken is cooked through.

While the chicken is cooking, make the couscous. Add the grains to the frying pan with the remaining sauce and bring to the boil. Cook for about 15 minutes, stirring regularly and keeping an eye on the grains to avoid overcooking. You may need to add a little boiling water if the liquid dries up towards the end of the cooking time.

Once everything is cooked, add the chicken, tarragon, shallots and any juices in the dish to the cooked couscous in the frying pan and stir to combine. Season to taste. Serve directly from the pan, scattered with the fresh parsley leaves and toasted pine nuts.

I am not, nor do I believe I will ever be, a vegetarian. I am, however, very aware of the changes happening in our society's meat consumption, and the effect eating meat has on the environment. Nowadays we are far more conscious of our diets, looking to vegetables as equally key – if not more important – ingredients than meat. I recommend having at least one day a week without meat – for both your health and that of the planet. The caraway seeds in this recipe bring a lot to the dish, so if possible, keep them in. The feta, however, can be swapped for something such as halloumi or even tofu. My father is a big meat lover and said of this recipe "I don't feel I am missing out anything", which made me grin from ear to ear. High praise indeed! Serve these burgers in buns with sliced avocado, crumbled feta, quick-pickled veg (chop up a red onion or some cucumber, cover with a little white or red wine vinegar and leave for 5 minutes), salad leaves and slices of tomato.

BEETROOT, CARAWAY AND FETA BURGERS

MAKES 4–6 LARGE BURGERS OR 8 SMALLER BURGERS

150–200g (5½–7oz) raw beetroot

1 large red onion

2 garlic cloves

1 teaspoon caraway seeds

½ teaspoon ground cumin

1 tablespoon olive oil, plus extra for frying

1 egg

125g (4½oz) feta cheese

75g (2¾oz) rolled oats

50g (1¾oz) flour (of any type you like), plus extra for dusting

salt and freshly ground black pepper

Begin by finely grating the beetroot, onion and garlic – the finer the better, as this gives the burgers a lighter texture. You could also use a food processor for this step. Put the grated veg in a bowl and season a little with salt and pepper, then add the spices, olive oil and egg. Mix to combine a bit, then crumble in the feta. Again, stir to combine, then add the oats and flour. If the mixture feels very wet, add a little more flour or oats. If it feels too dry, add a little water. It should be soft and easy to shape, but firm enough to hold the shape.

Divide the mixture into 4–6 equal portions, depending on the size of burgers you want, and shape them into flat rounds. Dust the patties with a little flour.

Heat a little olive oil in a large frying pan over a high heat. Once hot, add the burgers and immediately reduce the heat to medium. Cook for 2–3 minutes on each side or until lightly golden brown. Drain on kitchen paper, then serve.

If you are anything like me, you will smoke out the whole kitchen in the cooking process of this recipe. Fear not, though – the reward is great. All steaks are best when prepped and seasoned simply, cooked quickly and given plenty of time to rest. Do those three things and no amount of smoke will dampen the result. Serve these tasty strips of steak and the indulgent dips with some flatbread and a tangle of watercress.

STEAK WITH FEISTY GREEN OLIVE TAPENADE AND GARLIC MAYO

SERVES 4

2–4 sirloin steaks, about 750g
   (1lb 10oz) total weight
olive oil
1 teaspoon each of black and pink
   peppercorns, cracked
watercress, to serve

For the tapenade
200g (7oz) pitted green olives
1 small green chilli
juice of ½ lime
1 tablespoon white wine vinegar
2 tablespoons olive oil
small bunch of fresh coriander
salt and freshly ground black pepper

For the garlic mayo
2 smoked garlic cloves
2 tablespoons good olive oil
100g (3½oz) mayonnaise (see page
   268 for homemade)
smoked salt and freshly ground
   black pepper

Set a griddle pan over a high heat, ready to cook the steaks.

Lay out a large sheet of greaseproof paper and drizzle a little oil over half the paper. Sprinkle over some cracked pepper. Place the steaks on top in a single layer, then drizzle again with oil and sprinkle over some more pepper. Fold the greaseproof paper over to cover the steaks, like a book cover. Using a rolling pin or butcher's mallet, bash the meat all over through the top layer of greaseproof paper. You don't want to squash the meat flat, but make sure it has all been whacked firmly. This will improve the tenderness of the cooked meat.

Place one of the steaks on to your now-smoking-hot griddle pan and cook for 1½–2 minutes on each side, depending on the thickness of the steak. I would recommend medium-rare in this instance. Once cooked, set aside on a plate to rest and repeat with the remaining steaks, cooking them one at a time. Allow the cooked steaks to rest for at least 20 minutes, although the longer, the better.

To make the tapenade, place the ingredients in a food processor and blitz until you have a chunky paste. Season to taste.

For the mayo, mince the garlic in a mortar and pestle until you have a smooth paste, then add the oil and season with smoked salt and pepper. Stir your garlic oil into the mayonnaise until well mixed.

Slice the steaks into fine strips and serve with your 2 dips and sprigs of watercress.

This squid is gleefully quick to prepare and will be eaten even faster. All too often, squid is overcooked and rubbery, leaving people with distaste for it, but if that describes you, I urge you to give this recipe a go. By fast-frying squid, you achieve a crispy exterior with tender flesh inside. Serve the squid with this spiky salad for a kick of freshness.

SALT AND PEPPER SQUID

SERVES 2–4

300–450g (10½oz–1lb) cleaned squid
100g (3½oz) cornflour
100g (3½oz) plain flour
3 teaspoons ground black pepper
3 teaspoons ground pink pepper
sunflower or vegetable oil

For the salad and dressing
1 tablespoon rice wine vinegar
2 tablespoons olive oil
2 tablespoons lime juice
1 tablespoon clear honey
2 tablespoons white sesame seeds
½ cucumber, cut into fine ribbons
   with a vegetable peeler
3 spring onions, finely sliced into
   strips
1 green chilli, finely sliced into strips
small bunch of fresh coriander, leaves
   picked
punnet of cress, picked

Cut open the body of each squid and lay it out flat. Make small diagonal scores all along the surface, ensuring you don't cut all the way through. Slice the flesh into strips that are about 3cm (1¼ inches) thick – cut them horizontally so that the scores run diagonally down each strip. Leave the tentacles whole.

Heat a deep-fat fryer or a large saucepan with a good few inches of oil. You want the oil to reach a temperature of 180°C (350°F).

In a bowl, mix the flours and black and pink pepper together. Add the squid pieces to the flour mix and shake the bowl to coat the pieces well in the seasoned flour. Dust off any excess flour. You will need to cook the squid in batches, as you don't want to overcrowd the deep-fat fryer or saucepan. Slip the squid pieces into the oil. Fry for no more than 2 minutes until golden brown. Use a spider skimmer to remove the pieces and transfer to a plate lined with kitchen paper to drain.

To make the salad dressing, whisk the vinegar, oil, lime juice, honey and sesame seeds together until smooth.

Put the cucumber ribbons into a bowl with the spring onions, chilli and coriander leaves. Toss the salad together and dress just before serving with the squid and a good scattering of cress.

This recipe was inspired by a salad I once ate, but I have no memory of where or when it was. I simply remember it was pretty bloomin' tasty. I call for the parsley stems to be chopped and added to the dressing, and the fat from the bird to be used for an especially crispy crouton. Waste not, want not.

DUCK SALAD WITH POACHED EGGS

❉

SERVES 4

1 duck, about 2kg (4lb 8oz)
4 eggs
salt and freshly ground black pepper

For the croutons

1 ciabatta, torn into bite-sized pieces
6 garlic cloves
100g (3½oz) pumpkin seeds
50g (1¾oz) sunflower seeds
50g (1¾oz) white sesame seeds
100g (3½oz) walnuts pieces
100g (3½oz) Gorgonzola cheese
  (optional)

For the salad and dressing

3 spring onions, finely sliced
1 large bag of lamb's lettuce
small bunch of flat leaf parsley, leaves
  picked, stems very finely chopped
4 tablespoons olive oil
1 tablespoon red wine vinegar
1 teaspoon Dijon mustard
salt and freshly ground black pepper

Preheat the oven to 170°C (340°F), Gas Mark 3½.

Sit the duck on a rack in a deep roasting tray and season with salt and pepper. Roast for 1¾–2 hours.

Roughly 30 minutes before the duck is cooked, you can begin to assemble the other elements. Put the torn bread into a bowl. Leaving the skins on the garlic, bash the cloves using a pestle and mortar and add the pulp to the bowl with the seeds and nuts.

Remove the duck from the oven and spoon out and reserve some of the duck fat that has collected at the bottom of the tray. You will need around 4–5 tablespoons. Return the duck to the oven and add the hot fat to the bread bowl. Toss it through, then tip the mixture on to a baking tray. Bake for 7–10 minutes or until the bread is crunchy and the nuts and seeds are toasted.

Put the spring onions in a bowl with the salad and parsley leaves and carefully toss the onions through the leaves.

Make a dressing by whisking together the oil, vinegar, mustard and a little seasoning. Stir in the chopped parsley stems.

Bring a pan of water to the boil. Crack in 2 of the eggs, then reduce the heat to bring the water to a simmer and cover. Poach the eggs for 2–3 minutes. Remove the poached eggs with a slotted spoon, cover to keep them warm and set aside. Repeat with the remaining 2 eggs.

When the duck is cooked, shred the meat with 2 forks and, while it is still hot, combine with the toasted seedy bread and leaves. Dress the mixture, then divide it into bowls. Top with a crumbling of Gorgonzola, if using, and a poached egg.

Strain any leftover duck fat, removing the meat juices, and store it in a jar, refrigerated, for roast potatoes another day. It will keep for a few months.

*People are often daunted by artichokes and the prep that goes into them.
My first attempt at this recipe was in the French Alps, sitting in the pouring
rain surrounded by artichoke leaves and the inner fluff. It was stressful to
say the least (the barbecue was relit multiple times), but 2 hours later I sat
down to a mountain of the beautiful flowers and all was forgiven. It is a
simple method once you know how, just make sure you have plenty
of lemon water close by. Serve with some good bread and meats.*

CHARGRILLED ARTICHOKES WITH PARSLEY AND ANCHOVY SALAD

SERVES 4–6

1 large lemon
4–6 globe artichokes
2 tablespoons olive oil

For the salad and dressing
large bunch of flat leaf parsley, leaves
  picked, stems finely chopped
75g (2¾oz) rocket
50g (1¾oz) can anchovies in olive oil
finely grated zest and juice of 1 lemon
75g (2¾oz) pitted black olives, halved
olive oil
I teaspoon Dijon mustard
50g (1¾oz) Parmesan cheese (or any
  hard cheese of your choice), shaved
  or coarsely grated
edible flowers (optional)
salt and freshly ground black pepper

Begin by juicing half the lemon – reserve the squeezed-out rind. Add the juice to a large bowl of cold water.

To prep the artichokes, begin at the bottom of the "head". Clip the tough leaves off one by one, working your way up until the softer yellow flesh is visible. Then cut the greener top off so that you have only a yellow head. When you cut off the top, the bright purple centre should be visible. Cut the artichoke in half. Working quickly, rub the remaining lemon half over the now-exposed yellow flesh where you made the cut. This will prevent it from browning. Scrape out the purple and furry "choke" from the centre using a teaspoon. You should be left with a cup shape. Squeeze a little lemon juice into the centre, then submerge the whole thing into the prepared lemon water. Repeat with the remaining artichokes.

Once all the artichokes are prepped, you need to boil them. Tip the lemon water, artichokes and the reserved squeezed-out lemon rind into a deep saucepan and cook over a high heat for 10 minutes or until a knife can cut the artichokes easily. Drain in a sieve and leave to stand for a few moments to allow the artichokes to dry off a little (it won't take long, as they will be hot).

Preheat a griddle pan over a high heat until screaming hot. Brush the artichokes with the olive oil and char them on the hot griddle pan (or on a hot barbecue) for roughly 5 minutes until they are slightly blackened.

To prepare the salad, put the parsley leaves and the rocket into a bowl. Drain the anchovies, reserving the oil in a jar. Finely chop the anchovies and add them to the bowl with the lemon zest and olives.

Add the lemon juice to the anchovy oil in the jar with a splash of olive oil, the chopped parsley stems and the mustard. Place the lid on the jar and shake vigorously. Season to taste. Add the grated or shaved cheese to the greens along with the edible flowers, if using, then toss the dressing through the salad. Serve immediately with the chargrilled artichokes.

A sprinkling of Parmesan makes these fries extra crispy, so you can avoid the deeply unhealthy deep-frying method that usually produces this appealing result. A big paper cone of crispy fries with a tangle of greens and a silky pool of good mayo could turn around even the worst of days in no time at all.

SWEET POTATO AND PARMESAN FRIES

SERVES 4–6

about 1kg (2lb 4oz) sweet potatoes
8–10 garlic cloves
good glug of olive oil
pinch of salt
2 sprigs of rosemary, leaves stripped
50g (1¾oz) Parmesan cheese,
   finely grated

To serve
mayonnaise (see page 268 for
   homemade)
sea salt flakes

Preheat the oven to 190°C (375°F), Gas Mark 5.

Wash the sweet potatoes, but don't peel them (I like all my chips with the skins on). Cut each potato in half lengthways, then into 1cm (½ inch) thick chips.

Smash the garlic cloves with a flat side of your knife blade, keeping the skins on.

In a bowl, toss the chips together with the smashed garlic and the oil. Add the salt and ensure the chips are well coated. Tip them on to a roasting tray and arrange them in a single layer. Bake for 30 minutes.

Bring the chips out of the oven and carefully use a fish slice to loosen them from the tray. Sprinkle the rosemary and Parmesan all over and shake the tray to combine. Return to the oven for 3–5 minutes to allow the Parmesan to become crispy. Serve sprinkled with sea salt flakes and with a bowl of good mayo alongside.

SUMMER RIVER PICNIC

LEMON GRASS CORDIAL * *see page 211*

MACKEREL PATE * *see page 75*

LANGOUSTINES WITH AIOLI * *see page 183*

CHARGRILLED ARTICHOKES WITH PARSLEY
AND ANCHOVY SALAD * *see page 105*

GOOSEBERRY CAKE * *see page 132*

From left to right: Chargrilled artichokes with parsley and anchovy salad; Mackerel pâté; Gooseberry cake; Langoustines with aioli; Lemon grass cordial.

EVERYTHING BAKED

For a year and a half I worked in a lovely little tearoom in the middle of nowhere, halfway up a glen. It was hard graft but, in many respects, my dream job. We got a good reputation, so summers were chaotic and we often worked 12-hour shifts, yet still, it seemed we couldn't bake fast enough! But during the autumn and winter the pace would change. We would pad about making big hearty soups, cakes and soda bread, stopping to speak to the regulars that had braved the weather to visit us. The owner, a good family friend, is from the Isle of Barra and so we would refer to this time of year as "island pace". I was working with all my childhood friends and we did nothing but bake, blether and eat. Whenever I make soda bread now, I think back fondly to that wee café in the hills and of cooking, making coffee and looking out on to snowy mountains.

BALSAMIC ONION SODA BREAD

MAKES 1 LARGE OR 2 SMALL

2 large white onions or 3 banana
   shallots, finely sliced
3 tablespoons balsamic vinegar
20g (¾oz) caster sugar
450g (1lb) self-raising flour, plus extra
   for dusting
½ teaspoon bicarbonate of soda
250ml (9fl oz) milk
100g (3½oz) natural yogurt

Preheat the oven to 180°C (350°F) Gas Mark 4.

Put the sliced onions into a deep saucepan with the vinegar and sugar and cook over a medium-low heat for about 15 minutes. You are looking to soften the onions, then almost caramelize them. There should be no excess liquid in the pan.

While this is happening, weigh out the flour, bicarb, milk and yogurt into a large bowl to prepare the bread mixture.

Once the onions are ready, slide the pan off the heat and allow to cool for 5 minutes.

Stir the bread mixture together gently until just combined, then stir through the onions. Again, do not overmix – you just need to ensure the onions are evenly dispersed.

Generously dust a baking tray with flour, then tip the dough on top. Shape your bread, dusting your hands with the flour from the tray to avoid sticking – you are looking for a traditional round. Score the round into quarters.

Bake for 30 minutes. Your bread should be golden brown and hollow-sounding when tapped on the underside. Allow to cool completely for neat slices or, if you are feeling greedy, tuck in straight away, slathering the bread with good salted butter.

This tart is a beautiful fresh spring bake. It is much lighter than a traditional quiche due to the mixture of ricotta and crème fraîche. You can use dried herbs, but I really recommend having pots of fresh ones dotted around the house. They are easy to maintain and really lift dishes like this. The pastry can be used in any savoury tart or quiche for something a bit different to a regular shortcrust.

ASPARAGUS AND RICOTTA TART
WITH HERB PASTRY

SERVES 6–8

For the pastry
100g (3½oz) cold unsalted butter, cubed
150g (5½oz) plain flour, plus extra for dusting
40g (1½oz) wholemeal flour
10g (¼oz) cornflour
2 teaspoons chopped fresh herbs (such as basil, thyme and sage)
2–4 tablespoons milk
salt and freshly ground black pepper

For the filling
250g (9oz) asparagus, chopped diagonally into thirds
100g (3½oz) peas or shelled broad beans
200g (7oz) ricotta cheese
100ml (3½fl oz) milk
100g (3½oz) crème fraîche
2 eggs
3 tablespoons chopped fresh herbs (such as parsley, chives, mint)
75g (2¾oz) spring onions, finely sliced
75g (2¾oz) Parmesan cheese, grated
50g (1¾oz) pine nuts
salt and freshly ground black pepper

For the garnish
chopped fresh herbs (such as purple basil, parsley and chives), optional

Put all the ingredients for the pastry bar the milk in a food processor. Blitz until combined, then blitz in the milk 1 tablespoon at a time. Alternatively, rub the butter into the flours until the mixture resembles fine breadcrumbs, stir in the herbs, gradually add the milk, then knead gently until the mixture comes together. Once the pastry dough is smooth, wrap it in clingfilm and refrigerate for a minimum of 15 minutes.

Meanwhile, preheat the oven to 180°C (350°F), Gas Mark 4.

Bring a pan of water to the boil and cook the asparagus pieces for no more than 3 minutes. Scoop them out of the water and immediately plunge them into a bowl of cold water. Cook the peas or broad beans in the same water for no more than 1 minute. Drain and add these to the cold water.

In a bowl, whisk the ricotta, milk, crème fraîche, eggs, herbs and some seasoning together.

Roll out the pastry dough on a lightly floured work surface to a thickness of 2–3mm (1/16–1/8 inch). Transfer the dough to a 23cm (9 inch) loose-bottomed tart tin and gently press it into the edges of the tin. Run the rolling pin across the top edges of the tin to cut away the overhanging pastry.

Drain the vegetables and pat them dry. Scatter the sliced spring onion over the pastry with half the grated Parmesan. Now add the vegetables, reserving a few of the asparagus tips. Carefully pour the egg mixture on top. Don't worry if the vegetables all move around – this is fine. Top with the remaining grated cheese, the pine nuts and the reserved asparagus tips. Bake for 35–45 minutes until the filling is set and the pastry is golden brown. Garnish with a sprinkling of chopped fresh herbs, then serve.

I love the soothing combination of apple and oats together and I am often found grating Braeburns into porridge or making hearty orchard cakes with oat flour. These scones are lighter than your classic cheese scone and make a lovely accompaniment to a nice bowl of pea soup when they are hot out of the oven and served with good salted butter. Or serve them cold with some cream cheese mixed with lemon and pepper topped with chopped chives and a few slices of cucumber for a nice afternoon-tea treat.

APPLE, CHEDDAR AND OAT SCONES

MAKE 12 WEE SCONES

125g (4½oz) unsalted butter, cubed
450g (1lb) self-raising flour,
  plus extra for dusting
50g (1¾oz) rolled oats, plus extra
  for sprinkling
50g (1¾oz) Cheddar cheese, grated
1 apple, grated (I use a sharp dessert
  apple, such as Granny Smith)
125g (4½oz) natural yogurt
75ml (2½fl oz) milk, plus extra
  for brushing
2 eggs
salt and freshly ground black pepper

Preheat the oven to 220°C (425°F), Gas Mark 7.

Rub the butter into the flour and oats until the mixture forms a crumb-like texture. Stir in the grated cheese and apple. Season lightly.

In a jug or bowl, whisk the yogurt, milk and eggs together until smooth, then stir the wet ingredients into the dry ingredients. Do this gently to avoid overworking the mixture. As soon as the dough comes together, tip it out on to a lightly floured work surface and pat it out until it is 3cm (1¼ inch) thick. Using a round 5cm (2 inch) cookie cutter (or any size you want), cut out the scones, gently rerolling and cutting the offcuts.

Transfer the rounds to a baking tray and brush with a little milk, then top each round with a sprinkling of oats. Bake for 12–15 minutes or until the scones are well risen and golden.

I spent a lot of time playing with lactose-free recipes for my flatmate when we first moved in together. I was unaware of just how much dairy I had been using in my baking, so I set about finding recipes that didn't require dairy products. If you are cooking for those with allergies, as much as possible follow recipes that don't call for the problem ingredient, rather than using substitutes or "pretend ingredients". This way the flavour and texture is less altered and no one feels as though they are missing out. The first batch of these biscuits went down a storm and so have (unusually) remained unaltered since then. They are sweetened with a little honey but have an overall savoury flavour and are perfect served with a salad or cheese, if you don't have any dairy issues. Alternatively, you can package them in cellophane bags and give them as gifts.

NUT AND SEED SAVOURY BISCOTTI

MAKES APPROXIMATELY 20

175g (6oz) wholemeal spelt flour
½ teaspoon baking powder
100g (3½oz) mixed whole nuts
   (I like almonds, hazelnuts and
   walnuts for this)
100g (3½oz) mixed seeds (I use
   pumpkin, sesame and poppy seeds)
50g (1¾oz) clear honey
50ml (2fl oz) olive oil, plus extra
   for greasing
2 eggs
salt and freshly ground black pepper

Preheat the oven to 180°C (350°F), Gas Mark 4. Grease a 900g (2lb) loaf tin or similar rectangular baking tin and line it with baking paper.

Put all the ingredients into a large bowl and stir together using a wooden spoon. Once the mixture is fully combined, tip it into your lined tin. Flatten the top using wet hands. Bake for 30 minutes.

Remove from the oven and allow the loaf to cool in the tin for 15 minutes. Remove the loaf from the tin, transfer it to a wire rack and leave to cool for a further 15 minutes. Meanwhile, preheat the oven once again to 180°C (350°F), Gas Mark 4.

Using a sharp serrated knife, slice the loaf into thin biscuits. Arrange these on a large baking tray. Return the biscotti to the oven for the second bake. Bake them for 10 minutes, then turn them over and return to the oven for a further 5 minutes until crisp. You are looking for the biscuits to dry out at this stage, although they will colour a little, too. Transfer to a wire rack and allow to cool completely. The biscuits will keep in an airtight container for 1 month.

This is a delicious loaf with a good crust and a soft interior. The beer adds a certain earthiness to the flavour, which develops beautifully when the bread is refrigerated overnight. The whipped butter is optional, but I find it terribly moreish and like to slather it on top of a hearty slice of the bread. Enjoy the bread with a good ale, some cheese, tasty cold meats and a nice dollop of chutney – you will be lucky if you have any bread left for toast in the morning.

SEED AND GRAIN BEER BREAD
WITH WHIPPED BUTTER

MAKES 1 LOAF

100g (3½oz) strong wholemeal
  bread flour
325g (11½oz) strong white bread
  flour, plus extra for dusting
50g (1¾oz) mixed grains (oats and
  cracked wheat work well)
50g (1¾oz) mixed seeds, such as
  pumpkin, sesame, sunflower or
  anything else you have to hand
7g sachet (2 teaspoons) salt
7g sachet (2 teaspoons) fast-action
  dried yeast
330ml (11½fl oz) pale ale
oil, for greasing

For the whipped butter
250g (9oz) very soft unsalted butter,
  cubed
large pinch of sea salt flakes,
  lightly ground

The evening before baking, place all the bread ingredients in a bowl. Mix them together, then tip the dough on to a work surface. Knead for 10–15 minutes or until the dough is smooth and elastic. Resist the temptation to add more flour as you work – lightly oil the work surface if you find that the dough is sticking to it. If you would rather use a stand mixer, knead the dough with the dough hook attachment for 5–10 minutes or until smooth and elastic. Place the dough in a lightly oiled bowl and cover with clingfilm. Leave at room temperature to rise for 1–2 hours or until doubled in size.

    Tip the dough back on to the work surface and shape it into a ball by gently pulling dough from the sides down towards one side of the ball and pulling this gently together to form a seam (this less attractive side will form the base of the bread). Try not to lose too much of the air formed in the dough while doing this, although you don't need to worry massively if you do. If you have a proving basket, dust this generously with flour and place the dough into it, with the gathered seam facing upwards. If not, simply place the dough on to a floured baking tray with the gathered seam facing downwards. Cover loosely with clingfilm and leave to prove in the refrigerator overnight. Ensure it is not cramped by surrounding items in the refrigerator, as the dough will grow in size.

Recipe continued overleaf

When you wake up the following day, preheat the oven to as high as it will go. If you have a cast-iron frying pan, place this in the oven at the same time. If not, use a sturdy baking tray, again heating it with the oven.

Meanwhile, remove the dough from the refrigerator and allow it to come up to room temperature for 15–20 minutes. Once the oven is ready, remove your hot baking surface and carefully transfer the dough on to it with the gathered seam facing down. Use a sharp knife to slash the top of the dough quickly in any pattern you want, then bake for 30 minutes or until the bread is dark in colour and hollow-sounding on the underside when tapped. Allow to cool completely before slicing.

If you are making the whipped butter, place the butter in the bowl of a stand mixer with the salt. It is important that the butter is really soft for this process. Use a whisk attachment and whip for 5–7 minutes or until ice white. Spoon the whipped butter into a bowl and keep at room temperature until ready to serve. Slather generously on top of the bread for one of the simplest pleasures.

Oat flour is best used fresh, so simply use the amount of oats to suit the quantity you need in your chosen recipe. This recipe can be used to make Blackcurrant Crumb Slices (see page 126) or Gooseberry Cake (see page 132).

OAT FLOUR

MAKES 500G (1LB 2OZ)

500g (1lb 2oz) rolled oats

Put the oats into a food processor and blitz on a high speed setting for 5 minutes or until you have a fine flour. Use on the day of making.

I make these bars when we have a bounty of berries and a craving for baking – it's another good recipe for using up overripe fruit. A mixture between a tray bake and a crumble, these bars are loaded with fruit and are all the sweeter for it. You can use any berries for these; just make sure you don't hold back. Raspberries and rhubarb is a favourite combo of mine for this recipe. Serve with ice cream or a nice spoonful of mascarpone or clotted cream.

BLACKCURRANT CRUMB SLICES

MAKES 10 BARS

125g (4½oz) unsalted butter, softened
125g (4½oz) caster sugar
2 eggs
125g (4½oz) self-raising flour
1 teaspoon vanilla bean paste
200g (7oz) blackcurrants
200g (7oz) blueberries
5 tablespoons demerara sugar

For the crumble
40g (1½oz) cold butter, cubed
40g (1½oz) caster sugar
75g (2¾oz) Oat Flour (see page 125)

Preheat the oven to 180°C (350°F), Gas Mark 4. Grease and line a deep 23cm (9 inch) square baking tin.

First, make the crumble. In a bowl, rub the cold butter into the sugar and oat flour to form a rough crumble. Refrigerate the mixture for at least 15 minutes to allow it to firm up. This can also be made in advance and kept in the fridge at this stage overnight.

For the base, beat the softened butter and sugar together in a bowl until light and fluffy. Add the eggs one at a time, adding 2 tablespoons flour with each addition (this will prevent the batter from splitting). Once the mixture is smooth, fold in the remaining flour and the vanilla bean paste. Spoon the mixture into the prepared tin and spread it out in an even layer. Top evenly with the berries, then the chilled crumble. Sprinkle over the demerara sugar to finish.

Bake for 35–40 minutes or until a knife inserted into the centre comes out clean (or with only fruit on it and no uncooked batter from the base layer). Allow to cool completely in the tin, then cut the slab into 10 bars, or into squares if you prefer. Store in an airtight container for up to 5 days.

These sugary, spicy star-shaped shortbread biscuits immediately make me think of the festive period (and, of course, I can't help but play on the fact that star anise are star-shaped). If you are not a fan of the liquorice undertones present in star anise, please feel free to substitute it with 1½ teaspoons of ground cinnamon or ginger or, a personal favourite, grated nutmeg. These shortbreads make lovely gifts when wrapped in little cellophane bags tied up with a pretty ribbon. You could make a hole towards the top of each star before baking, then use the holes to string the stars together for an alternative Christmas tree decoration – not just gorgeous, but also edible.

STAR ANISE SHORTBREAD STARS

❊

MAKES 25–30

5–7 star anise (only use 5 if they
    are large)
125g (4½oz) unsalted butter
100g (3½oz) light brown sugar
50g (1¾oz) golden syrup
300g (10½oz) plain flour, plus extra
    for dusting
½ teaspoon bicarbonate of soda

For the icing
200g (7oz) icing sugar
milk

Preheat the oven to 180°C (350°F), Gas Mark 4. Line a large baking sheet with baking paper.

In a spice grinder, blitz the star anise to a very fine powder. If you don't have a spice grinder, bash them using a pestle and mortar, but make sure you sieve the resulting powder to remove any pieces that remain woody.

To make the biscuits, melt the butter, sugar and syrup together in a large saucepan over a low heat – do not allow the mixture to boil. Stir in the flour, bicarb and ground star anise. Beat the mixture with a wooden spoon until a dough forms.

Transfer the dough to a lightly floured work surface and roll it out to a thickness of 5–7mm (¼–⅜ inch). Cut out small star shapes using a 5cm (2 inch) star-shaped cookie cutter. Transfer the shapes to the prepared baking sheet. Bake for 9–12 minutes or until golden. Leave the biscuits to cool on the baking sheet for 5 minutes, then transfer to a wire rack and leave to cool completely.

For the icing, mix the sugar together with a few drops of milk – you are looking for a fairly thick mixture. Transfer one-third of the icing to a piping bag fitted with fine round nozzle. Pipe a border around the edge of each star biscuit. Allow the icing to set for 5 minutes, then return any excess icing to the bowl. Now add a few more drops of milk to create a slightly runnier icing that will flood the centre of the biscuits – the border will contain the flood icing. Using a teaspoon, spread a little of the runny icing in the middle of a star biscuit. A cocktail stick is a handy tool at this stage to encourage the icing to run right up to the border in the corners. Once the entire star is covered, repeat with the remaining biscuits. (It is important that your outline is properly dried before you start using the flood icing, or you will have a messy finish.) Allow the icing to dry out completely. Store the shortbreads in an airtight container for up to 1 week.

I am lucky enough to have an abundance of gooseberries in the hedgerows along from our house and can venture out, come August, and fill a huge bucket in under 30 minutes. They are becoming much more readily available in shops, but if you can't source fresh ones, or they are out of season, I have made this cake successfully with canned gooseberries before. I love the tanginess of gooseberries with golden caster sugar, but you can go for light soft brown sugar instead and achieve a more complex sweetness. This cake is perfect with some clotted cream or yogurt for afternoon tea in the late summer sunshine. A wee slice with a hot cup of tea and some yogurt will brighten up any day.

GOOSEBERRY CAKE

SERVES 8–10

200g (7oz) very soft unsalted butter,
  plus extra for greasing
200g (7oz) golden caster sugar
4 large eggs
200g (7oz) plain flour
75g (2¾oz) soured cream
  or natural yogurt
100g (3½oz) Oat Flour (see page 125)
1 teaspoon baking powder
1 teaspoon vanilla bean paste
300g (10½oz) gooseberries
5 tablespoons demerara sugar

Preheat the oven to 180°C (350°F), Gas Mark 4. Grease a 20cm (8 inch) round loose-bottomed cake tin and line it with baking paper.

In a bowl, beat the butter and caster sugar together until light and fluffy. Beat in the eggs one at a time, adding 2 tablespoons plain flour with each addition (this will prevent the batter from splitting). Once all the eggs are added, stir in the soured cream. Once combined, fold in the remaining plain flour, the oat flour and baking powder. When the mixture is smooth, stir in the vanilla and 200g (7oz) of the gooseberries. Spoon the batter into the prepared tin, then top with the remaining berries and sprinkle over the demerara sugar.

Bake for 45–50 minutes or until a knife inserted into the centre of the cake comes out clean. Allow to cool in the tin for 5 minutes, then transfer to a wire rack and leave to cool completely.

A twist on the humble carrot cake. These little sponges are made in a similar fashion to their famous cousin, but have a much more complex flavour that is almost honey-like. The benefit of using vegetables in cakes is not only the moistness they provide but also that you achieve a sweeter and earthier flavour. When vegetables are cooked at a fairly low heat, the natural sugar (no matter how little there is) comes out and enhances everything. All good things, in my opinion.

PARSNIP AND COCONUT CAKES

MAKES 12

150ml (¼ pint) sunflower oil
150ml (¼ pint) coconut oil, melted (or use 150ml/¼ pint extra sunflower oil)
300g (10½oz) light brown sugar
300g (10½oz) parsnips, peeled and grated
1 teaspoon ground ginger
finely grated zest of ½ lemon
3 eggs
300g (10½oz) self-raising flour

For the icing and decoration
150g (5½oz) unsalted butter, softened
300g (10½oz) icing sugar
100ml (3½fl oz) coconut cream
200g (7oz) coconut flakes

Preheat the oven to 180°C (350°F), Gas Mark 4. Line a 12-hole muffin tin with paper cases.

In a bowl, whisk the oils and sugar together. Add the grated parsnip, ginger, lemon zest and eggs and mix again until smooth. Fold in the flour. Use an ice-cream scoop to divide the mixture between the paper cases in the tin – you want to fill the cases three-quarters of the way up. (Reserve any excess batter.) Bake for 20–25 minutes until golden and springy to touch. Leave to cool in the tin for 5 minutes, then transfer to a wire rack and leave to cool completely. (Repeat the process if you have any excess batter.)

To make the icing, beat the butter and sugar together until very pale and smooth. Stir the coconut cream into the icing gently, being careful not to overmix it. You should have a spreadable and light icing. Dollop a tablespoon of icing on top of each cake and smooth it over the top surface with a knife, then finish with a sprinkling of the coconut flakes.

This is one of those cakes that came about quite haphazardly and with little expectation. Having spent a morning experimenting with various nut and seed butters, I was in the mood for something sweet. Figs were in the fruit bowl, so I thought they must be included, but I was stumped as to what else to add. And so, in a carefree fashion, I chucked some excess almond butter into a loaf, whacked it in the oven and walked away. To my delight, the result was pretty special, so this is a recipe that I have been making ever since.

FIG AND ALMOND LOAF

SERVES 10

225g (8oz) unsalted butter, softened,
  plus extra for greasing
175g (6oz) light brown sugar
50g (1¾oz) caster sugar
1 teaspoon vanilla bean paste
4 eggs
225g (8oz) self-raising flour
125g (4½oz) Almond Butter (see below)

For the almond butter
150g (5½oz) whole blanched almonds
50ml (2fl oz) oil (melted coconut
  or vegetable)

For the icing and decoration
50g (1¾oz) unsalted butter, softened
125g (4½oz) icing sugar
50g (1¾oz) Almond Butter (see above)
3–4 figs, quartered
50g (1¾oz) whole blanched almonds,
  toasted

Preheat the oven to 180°C (350°F), Gas Mark 4. Grease a 900g (2lb) loaf tin and line it with baking paper.

Begin with the nut butter. (If making your own, I recommend doubling or even tripling the quantities, as it will keep for ages.) Toast the nuts on a baking tray in the oven for 3–4 minutes or until fragrant and very light brown in colour (you can toast the 50g/1¾oz almonds to be used for decorating at the same time). Allow to cool for 5 minutes, then transfer to a food processor and blitz for 7–10 minutes. Stop to scrape down the sides of the bowl once or twice. When you have a smooth paste, add the oil and blitz again until smooth.

To make the batter, beat the butter and sugars together in a bowl until light and fluffy. Beat in the vanilla, then add the eggs one at a time, adding 2 tablespoons of the flour with each addition (this will prevent the batter from splitting). Fold in the remaining flour until the mixture is smooth, then gently stir in the almond butter. Spoon the batter into the prepared loaf tin. Bake for 45–60 minutes or until a knife inserted into the centre of the cake comes out clean. Leave to cool in the tin for 5 minutes, then remove from the tin and transfer to a wire rack to cool completely.

For the icing, beat the butter, sugar and the almond butter together in a bowl until smooth. Spread generously over the cooled loaf. Finish with the figs and more toasted almonds.

Adapted from the famous Italian yogurt pot cake, this wonderfully soft sponge has been made for years in our kitchen. If you want to go full-on raspberry, you can use a raspberry yogurt instead of plain, too. I adore the pops of pink with the little speckles of poppy seeds. You can ice this cake with a cream cheese frosting, but I prefer it with just a dusting of icing sugar and a little yogurt on the side.

YOGURT, POPPY SEED AND RASPBERRY CAKE

SERVES 8–10

150ml (¼ pint) vegetable oil
200g (7oz) caster sugar
2 eggs
150g (5½oz) natural yogurt
200g (7oz) self-raising flour
2 tablespoons poppy seeds
200g (7oz) raspberries
icing sugar, for dusting (optional)

Preheat the oven to 180°C (350°F), Gas Mark 4. Grease a 20cm (8 inch) round loose-bottomed cake tin and line it with baking paper.

In a bowl, whisk the oil, caster sugar, eggs and yogurt together. Once the mixture is smooth, add the flour and poppy seeds. Fold in the raspberries, then spoon the batter into your prepared tin.

Bake for 35–40 minutes or until a knife inserted into the centre of the cake comes out clean. Leave to cool in the tin for 5 minutes, then transfer to a wire rack and leave to cool completely. Dust with icing sugar to serve, if you like.

I only learnt to make these because I adored how they looked. I know that is not the best reason for learning a new recipe, but I saw them stacked high in a London bakery and before I had even tasted them I wanted to give making them a go. A few years later we met Jenny, a family friend from Sweden, who introduced me to cassia cinnamon, or Chinese cinnamon. It is the most common type of cinnamon used in Sweden (and the USA) and has a much sweeter flavour compared to the verum cinnamon we are used to in the UK. It reminds me a little of cardamom, and for that I love it. Cassia cinnamon is readily available online, but you can, of course, use regular store-cupboard cinnamon if you would prefer.

KANELBULLAR

**MAKES 12 LARGE
OR 18 SMALL**

300g (10½oz) plain flour, plus extra
    for dusting
7g sachet (2 teaspoons) fast-action
    dried yeast
100g (3½oz) caster sugar
175ml (6fl oz) milk, plus extra
    for brushing
1 egg
½ teaspoon salt
flaked almonds, to decorate
    (or use sugar pearls)

For the filling
100g (3½oz) unsalted butter, softened
50g (1¾oz) ground almonds
100g (3½oz) caster sugar
10g (¼oz) ground cassia cinnamon
½ teaspoon grated nutmeg
½ teaspoon ground cardamom
finely grated zest of 1 large orange

Put the flour, yeast, sugar, milk, egg and salt into the bowl of a stand mixer, adding the yeast and salt at opposite sides of the bowl. Using the dough hook attachment, knead for 5 minutes until the dough is smooth and elastic. Alternatively, mix the ingredients together in a bowl and knead on a lightly floured work surface for roughly 10 minutes, then place the dough in a bowl for rising. Cover the bowl with clingfilm and leave in a warm place to rise for 1 hour or until doubled in size.

Line a large baking tray with baking paper.

For the filling, in a mixing bowl, beat the butter, almonds and sugar together until smooth. Add the spices and orange zest and beat again.

Knock the dough back on to a lightly floured surface. Roll it out to form a 30 x 23cm (12 x 9 inch) rectangle. Spread the cinnamon filling evenly across half the rectangle so that a 15 x 23cm (6 x 9 inch) area is covered. Fold the uncovered half, like a book, over the filling, smooth over the top with your hands to press any trapped air bubbles out from the edges, then press the edges of the dough with your fingers to seal them.

Roll out to a 23 x 23cm (9 x 9 inch) square. Cut into 1cm (½ inch) strips (or for larger buns, cut 2.5cm/1 inch strips.). Take one strip and twist it to form a spiral. Next, roll the twisted strip tightly into a coil, then press the end underneath in the middle to secure. Place on the prepared baking tray and repeat with the remaining strips. You can form these into knots or coils or any way you like or even make a whole bun out of various coils instead of starting with a spiral. Set aside to prove for 25–30 minutes or until doubled in size.

Meanwhile, preheat the oven to 200°C (400°F), Gas Mark 6.

Brush each bun with a little milk, then sprinkle with the flaked almonds. Bake for 15–20 minutes (20–25 minutes for larger buns) until golden brown.

I am aware that it is deeply, deeply cruel of me to provide a brownie recipe that requires overnight chilling. I cannot recommend it enough, however. The result will be a very dark and dense fudgy slab of goodness with an all-important crunchy top. These brownies are particularly good as a pudding, served either hot or cold with ice cream. They also make lovely gifts when cut into teensy squares, dusted with edible gold lustre or gold leaf and wrapped prettily. Well worth the wait in my opinion.

COCOA NIB BROWNIES

MAKES 10–12

150g (5½oz) unsalted butter, plus
  extra for greasing
150g (5½oz) milk chocolate
100g (3½oz) dark chocolate
  (minimum 54% cocoa solids)
½ teaspoon sea salt flakes
100g (3½oz) caster sugar
150g (5½oz) light muscovado sugar
4 eggs
100g (3½oz) plain flour
3 tablespoons cocoa nibs
100g (3½oz) mixed nuts and seeds
  (I like almonds with black sesame
  and pumpkin seeds)

Preheat the oven to 160°C (325°F), Gas Mark 3. Grease and line a deep baking tin measuring roughly 23cm (9 inch) square.

Melt the butter and chocolates together in a large saucepan over a low heat to prevent the chocolate from burning and separating. Once fully combined, mix in the salt and sugar. Take the pan off the heat and allow the mixture to cool down for 5 minutes.

Once the mixture is no longer hot, add the eggs and flour. Mix together well. Scrape the batter into the prepared tin and spread it out into an even layer. Sprinkle the cocoa nibs, nuts and seeds evenly all over the surface.

Bake for 30–40 minutes or until a skewer inserted into the centre comes out sticky but not wet with liquid batter. Allow to cool in the tin fully, then cover the tin with clingfilm and refrigerate overnight to allow to set.

Cut into 10–12 squares, or any size you like.

A tasty twist on the classic. I defy anyone not to jump up and down a little when they spy a beautifully light sponge pilled high with cream and, in this case, a boozy pink strawberry compote. Serve, of course, with a generous glass of more Pimm's.

STRAWBERRY AND HIBISCUS
VICTORIA SPONGE

SERVES 8–10

200g (7oz) unsalted butter, softened,
  plus extra for greasing
200g (7oz) caster sugar
200g (7oz) white spelt or plain flour
1 teaspoon baking powder
4 eggs

For the filling and decoration
200g (7oz) strawberries, halved
1 tablespoon dried hibiscus flowers
2 tablespoons caster sugar
60ml (4 tablespoons) Pimm's
300ml (½ pint) double cream
1 teaspoon vanilla bean paste
2 tablespoons icing sugar, plus extra
  for dusting
non-toxic fresh flowers or rose petals,
  to decorate

Preheat the oven to 180°C (350°F), Gas Mark 4. Grease 2 x 20cm (8 inch) round loose-bottomed cake tins and line them with baking paper.

In a bowl, cream the butter and sugar together until very light and fluffy. In a separate bowl, mix the flour and baking powder together. Beat the eggs into the butter mix one at a time, adding 2 tablespoons of the flour with each egg and beating well between each addition. Fold in the remaining flour until the mixture is smooth. Divide the batter between the 2 prepared tins and level out the surfaces.

Bake for 25–30 minutes or until a knife inserted into the centre of each cake comes out clean. Allow the cakes to cool in the tins for 15 minutes, then transfer to a wire rack to cool completely.

While the cakes are cooling, make the filling. Put the strawberries, hibiscus flowers, caster sugar and Pimm's into a saucepan and bring to a very gentle boil over a medium-low heat, stirring continuously. Cook gently for about 10 minutes until the mixture has reduced slightly, to the consistency of a loose jam. Take the pan off the heat and set aside to allow the filling mixture to cool. Remove and discard the hibiscus petals once cold.

When ready to assemble the cake, whip the cream, vanilla and icing sugar together in a bowl to form very soft peaks. Place one cake on a cake stand or plate, then spread the cream generously on top. Spoon the strawberry mixture over the top surface and drizzle with the juices. Place the second cake on top and dust with icing sugar. Decorate with flowers or a few rose petals. Serve immediately.

I don't think the Empire biscuit is as popular anywhere else as it is in Scotland. They are sold in most wee bakeries – you would struggle to walk more than 500 yards in Glasgow without seeing one for sale. As a kid I was only in it for the sweetie on the top (I have an uncle who adores Empire biscuits, so this was never an issue), but nowadays I love the whole thing. This version omits the jelly tot (I can only apologize) in favour of a more floral and slightly prettier theme. It is very much a floral Flora creation. I would highly recommend making the Strawberry and Elderflower Jam (see page 258) for this recipe, but you can, of course, use whichever berry jam takes your fancy. Simply make sure it is a fairly thick one so that it won't come oozing out the sides.

FLORAL EMPIRE BISCUITS

MAKES 24–30

For the biscuits
225g (8oz) plain flour, plus extra
   for dusting
175g (6oz) unsalted butter, cubed
75g (2¾oz) icing sugar
1 teaspoon vanilla bean paste
1 teaspoon dried elderflowers,
   rose petals or lavender (optional)

For the icing
200g (7oz) icing sugar
milk

For the filling and decoration
50g (1¾oz) mixed dried edible flower
   petals (I use dried rose, cornflower
   and marigold petals)
200g (7oz) raspberry jam or
   Strawberry and Elderflower Jam
   (see page 258)

Preheat the oven to 180°C (350°F), Gas Mark 4. Line a large baking sheet with baking paper.

To make the biscuits, blitz the flour, butter, sugar, vanilla and dried flowers in a food processor until a dough forms. Alternatively, rub the butter into the other ingredients and knead by hand until you achieve a dough.

Roll out the dough on a lightly floured work surface until it has the thickness of a pound coin. Use a fluted round cookie cutter to cut out the biscuits, then reroll the scraps and repeat. You should get 24–30 biscuits, depending on your size of cutter. Transfer the shapes to the prepared baking sheet. Bake for 12–15 minutes or until just beginning to turn golden. Leave the biscuits to cool on the baking sheet for 5 minutes, then transfer to a wire rack and leave to cool completely.

For the icing, mix the sugar with a splash of milk in a bowl until you have a thickish icing – it should be spreadable. Transfer to a piping bag fitted with a round nozzle.

To assemble the biscuits, pipe a circle of the icing on top of half the biscuits. While the icing is still wet, sprinkle with some of the petals. Dollop a teaspoon of jam on the underside of each of the remaining half of the biscuits, then sandwich together with the decorated halves on top. Allow the icing to set fully. These biscuits are best eaten on the day of making, as the jam tends to soften them after 24 hours. You can, however, bake the biscuits up to 3 days in advance of serving and assemble them in the morning of the day they are required.

When I was 14, I applied for a work experience placement in the wardrobe department at Pitlochry Festival Theatre. Much to my delight they said yes, and so I headed up the A9 for a week of stitching, sizing and tea-sipping. I completely and utterly adored it. Two weeks later, I got home from school to a note on the table asking me to "call the dress ladies". They offered me a Saturday job and I didn't leave again for two years, working on pantos and the busy summer season. On my 16th birthday, the lovely Iona made me a Guinness cake. It was completely delicious and felt even more indulgent considering the fact that I had never even tasted Guinness before. I am now aware that its proper title is Black Velvet Cake, which makes it even more fitting for my work as a seamstress, but I think it will forever be wardrobe cake to me.

WARDROBE CAKE

SERVES 8–10

250g (9oz) unsalted butter, plus extra
  for greasing
300ml (½ pint) Guinness
100g (3½oz) dark chocolate
  (minimum 54% cocoa solids)
50g (1¾oz) cocoa powder
300g (10½oz) self-raising flour
300g (10½oz) caster sugar
2 eggs
100ml (3½fl oz) double cream
1 teaspoon vanilla bean paste

For the icing and decoration
150g (5½oz) unsalted butter, softened
150g (5½oz) icing sugar
200g (7oz) cream cheese
50g (1¾oz) good-quality white
  chocolate, curls or grated (optional)

Preheat the oven to 180°C (350°F), Gas Mark 4. Grease a 20cm (8 inch) round loose-bottomed cake tin and line it with baking paper.

Put the butter, Guinness, chocolate and cocoa into a large saucepan set over a low heat until the butter and chocolate have just melted and no more – do not let the mixture boil. Then stir in the flour and caster sugar. Once combined, add the eggs, cream and vanilla.

Pour the batter into your prepared tin and bake for 45–50 minutes or until a knife inserted into the centre of the cake comes out clean. Allow to cool in the tin for 15 minutes, then transfer to a wire rack and leave to cool completely.

To make the icing, beat the butter and icing sugar together in a bowl until pale and fluffy. Add the cream cheese and beat again for 1 minute. Cut the top of the cake to level it if required, then spoon the icing on to the top of the cake and spread it across the surface to the edges. Decorate with the white chocolate, if you like.

- MENU -
GARDEN PARTY

PIMM'S * *see page 205*

RAINBOW RICE PAPER ROLLS * *see page 91*

APPLE, CHEDDAR AND OAT SCONES * *see page 119*

STRAWBERRY AND HIBISCUS VICTORIA SPONGE * *see page 143*

FLORAL EMPIRE BISCUITS * *see page 144*

PEACH AND RASPBERRY ICE LOLLIES * *see page 233*

From left to right: Pimms; Strawberry &and hibiscus Victoria sponge; Apple, Cheddar and oat scones.

FOOD TO TAKE YOUR TIME ABOUT

I met Regina when we were on holiday in Italy three years ago. I had never been to Italy before and fell ungracefully head over heels for the food. Not the Anglicized Italian food we get here, but the proper fresh, simple stuff, like figs off the tree in the garden and pasta made by the lovely Regina. One morning, I sheepishly asked her if she would teach me, and an hour later I was in her kitchen making passata, tagliatelle and cavatelli. The entire family then came and tucked in before heading back out to the farm in the baking heat. But I hurried back to my room and transferred the rough notes I had taken on Post-it notes to my book and wrote up a full recipe. Since then, I have used that exact same recipe and it has not failed me once. Regina, you are the sweetest. Thank you.

REGINA'S BASIC PASTA DOUGH

MAKES 700G (1LB 9OZ)

500g (1lb 2oz) *grano duro* or 00 flour,
   plus extra for dusting
5 eggs
2½ tablespoons white wine

In a stand mixer or food processor, blitz all the ingredients until smooth. You want the dough to be very smooth, so it will take about 8–10 minutes. Even Regina made the dough in this way, but you can, of course, knead it by hand.

Split the dough into 2 equal portions and wrap them in clingfilm. Allow to sit at room temperature for 30–60 minutes. This relaxes the dough – after this sitting time, you should notice it will spring back gently when prodded.

Cut one of the dough portions in half and re-cover one half with clingfilm. On a floured work surface, begin to roll out the dough. It will take about 5 minutes of rolling to achieve the right thinness. There are two tricks to tell if the dough is ready or not. The first is to place the dough on top of a sheet of newspaper – you should be able to read the small text easily. The second trick is to bend down until you are level with the work surface. Blow between the pasta and the worktop, and if the pasta ripples and wafts gently away like a fine piece of paper would, it's ready. Cut the dough into thin or thick strips – you can even shape these into bows for farfalle. Place the shapes on a large baking tray dusted with more flour. Repeat with the remaining dough, always covering any you're not using. Set aside to dry for 1 hour.

This recipe makes a large quantity of pasta, so once all the pasta has dried for an hour, you can cook half now and leave the rest to dry for a further hour or so to cook sometime in the next few days.

I made these pasta parcels for my parents' 20th wedding anniversary after discovering that they were often served at traditional Italian weddings. I am a sucker for a tradition, and also for anything that involves squash, nutmeg and sage. Although fun to make, they are a bit of a faff to shape, so don't worry if you want to adapt the shaping slightly and simply make a regular tortellini.

WEDDING PARCELS
(TORTELLI PIACENTINI)

SERVES 2–4

semolina, for dusting
½ quantity Regina's Basic Pasta
    Dough (see page 154 – use 2 whole
    eggs and 1 yolk)
1 egg white, beaten
100g (3½oz) unsalted butter
bunch of fresh sage, leaves picked and
    roughly chopped
100g (3½oz) whole blanched
    hazelnuts, toasted and chopped

For the filling

350g (12oz) butternut squash,
    peeled deseeded and cut into
    2cm (¾ inch) dice
2 tablespoons olive oil
2 sprigs of rosemary, leaves stripped
50g (1¾oz) cream cheese
50g (1¾oz) breadcrumbs
50g (1¾oz) Parmesan cheese, grated
½ teaspoon freshly grated nutmeg

Preheat the oven to 200°C (400°F), Gas Mark 6.

To make the filling, put the squash into a roasting tray with the oil and rosemary. Roast for 25–30 minutes or until the squash is soft.

Transfer the squash to a food processor and blitz until smooth. Add the cream cheese, breadcrumbs, Parmesan and nutmeg and blitz to a thick purée. Transfer the mixture to a piping bag fitted with a round nozzle.

Spread a thick layer of semolina over a tray and set to one side. Roll out the pasta as per the instructions on page 154. Cover the sheets so that they don't dry out. Using a cookie cutter, cut out 7–10 circles that are 8–9cm (3¼–3½ inches) across – don't cut out more than this in one go, or they will dry out before you have had the chance to form them. Starting in the middle of a pasta circle, pipe a long upside-down triangle on to the bottom two-thirds of the round, leaving a 3mm (⅛ inch) rim on the bottom and a 2cm (¾ inch) rim on the sides. Brush any exposed pasta with a little egg white. Fold in the bottom sides of the pasta so that they overlap the long triangle edges. You should have a cone shape with a round top. Now fold one side of the cone over the filling and then the other side, pinching in between. Repeat this to form a plait like effect. At the top, pinch the whole parcel together – don't worry if some filling leaks out; just ensure it is sealed at the end of the shaping process. Place the finished parcel on the tray of semolina. Repeat with the remaining discs. Cut out more discs and continue until you run out of filling. (The pasta scraps can be re-rolled for making spaghetti.)

To cook the pasta, bring a large pan of salted water to the boil. Adding the parcels in batches, cook for no more than 3 minutes.

Put the butter and sage into a large saucepan set over a low heat and melt the butter. Once it begins to foam, add the pasta and chopped hazelnuts and coat well. Serve immediately.

One of the beautiful things about making your own pasta is the versatility of it – you can tease it into any shape you could possible want. However, when I first rolled out sheets and sheets of my own, I simply wanted to cook them as they were: soft, silky handkerchiefs. This recipe takes the essence of a lasagne but speeds up the process a bit. The result is a celebration of pure and simple pasta, and hopefully one that would make even an Italian proud.

RIBBON LASAGNE

❄

SERVES 4

flour, for dusting
5 large tomatoes
handful of cherry tomatoes,
3 small red onions
1 red pepper, cored and deseeded
1 yellow pepper, cored and deseeded
1 courgette
1 aubergine
6 garlic cloves
2 tablespoons olive oil
2 tablespoons balsamic vinegar
½ quantity Regina's Basic Pasta
    Dough (see page 154 – use 2 whole
    eggs and 1 yolk)
75g (2¾oz) Parmesan cheese,
    finely grated
3–4 sprigs of fresh thyme, leaves
    picked
salt and freshly ground black pepper
frisée salad, to serve

For the whipped ricotta
100g (3½oz) ricotta
100g (3½oz) cream cheese
50ml (2fl oz) milk

Preheat the oven to 180°C (350°F), Gas Mark 4.

Roughly chop all the veggies into similar-sized chunks – the cherry tomatoes can remain whole. Bash the garlic cloves with the skins on. Chuck everything into a deep roasting tray and drizzle with the oil and vinegar. Roast for 1 hour.

While the veg are roasting, roll out the pasta. You are looking for sheets of pasta that are essentially large rectangles. Once rolled, dust with more flour and allow to dry for 20 minutes.

In a bowl, whisk the ricotta and cream cheese together for about 5 minutes until light and smooth in texture. Add the milk and season to taste. Whisk again. Stir half the grated Parmesan into the ricotta mixture.

When you are ready to serve, bring a large pan of boiling water to the boil, then cook the pasta sheets for 1–2 minutes. Drain, then immediately add the sheets to the roasting tin of veggies. Add a few spoonfuls of the starchy water to the tray as well, as this will help loosen the sauce. Fold the pasta through so that you create little pockets of pasta filled with veg. Sprinkle with the thyme leaves and the remaining Parmesan and return to the oven for 5 minutes. Serve with the whipped ricotta and some frisée leaves.

I love the addition of celeriac in this recipe, as I often find gratins quite heavy going. The celeriac adds a lovely earthy tone to the proceedings that helps combat the vats of dairy involved in this recipe. It is certainly a comforting winter number!

CELERIAC GRATIN

❋

SERVES 4–6

750g (1lb 10oz) potatoes, peeled

2 banana shallots

1 large (roughly 750g/1lb 10oz) celeriac, peeled

450ml (16fl oz) double cream

150g (5½oz) crème fraîche

50g (1¾oz) Gruyère cheese, grated, plus extra to top

50g (1¾oz) Parmesan cheese, grated

2 garlic cloves, finely chopped or minced

1 teaspoon freshly grated nutmeg

salt and freshly ground black pepper

50g (1¾oz) unsalted butter, softened

small bunch of fresh thyme, leaves stripped

cracked black peppercorns

Preheat the oven to 190°C (375°F), Gas Mark 5.

Using a mandoline, finely slice the potatoes, shallots and celeriac.

In a jug, whisk the cream and crème fraîche together. Whisk in the grated cheeses, minced garlic, nutmeg and seasoning, mixing well.

Grease a ceramic baking dish with the butter, then break up any excess butter into little pieces and whisk these into the cream mixture.

Arrange half the potato slices in the base of the prepared dish. Pour over roughly a quarter of the cream mixture. Next, arrange a layer of shallot using half the shallot slices, then a layer of half the celeriac slices. Add another quarter of the cream mixture. Repeat the process, finishing with the remaining cream mixture. Sprinkle over some extra grated Gruyère, the thyme leaves and the cracked black pepper, to taste. Bake for 1 hour or until golden brown, bubbling away and cooked through (a knife inserted into the middle will let you know if the potatoes are soft enough or not). Serve immediately by plonking the dish on the table and letting people dig in themselves.

I (quite embarrassingly) only discovered you could have pizzas without a tomato base when I went to Italy. We enjoyed a huge pizza of potato, rosemary and mozzarella in Tuscany, and were delighted by the freshness of flavour. It was a revelation. I have only made minor tweaks to the classic recipe here (if it ain't broke, don't fix it), but after our Tuscan treat I have made many variations and heartily recommend replacing the onion with a few sliced courgettes, some fresh thyme and finishing with rocket.

PIZZA BIANCO (OF SORTS)

MAKES 2 LARGE PIZZAS

For the pizza dough
450g (1lb) strong white bread flour, plus extra for dusting
7g sachet (2 teaspoons) fast-action dried yeast
10g (¼oz) salt
150ml (¼ pint) water
1 tablespoon clear honey
5 tablespoons olive oil, plus extra for greasing

For the topping
juice of 1 lemon
200g (7oz) cream cheese
1 red onion, very finely sliced (use a mandoline)
1 potato, peeled and very finely sliced (use a mandoline)
2–3 sprigs of rosemary, leaves stripped
50g (1¾oz) taleggio or mozzarella cheese, sliced or torn
olive oil, for drizzling
salt and freshly ground black pepper

To make the dough, mix all the ingredients together in a large bowl. Tip the dough out on to a lightly floured work surface and knead until very smooth and elastic. Put the dough in a lightly oiled bowl and cover with clingfilm. Allow to rise at room temperature until doubled in size – this will take 45–60 minutes.

Preheat the oven to the hottest setting possible and place 2 large baking trays, or pizza stones if you have them, in the oven to also heat up.

Once the dough has risen, knock it back on a lightly floured work surface. Knead it for a further minute, then divide it into 2 equal portions.

For the topping, beat the lemon juice with the cream cheese in a bowl until smooth, then season lightly.

Roll out the dough portions into rough, fairly thin rounds. Spread each one with half the cream cheese mixture, then divide the veg between them both. Sprinkle over the rosemary and finish with a little cheese. Add a little black pepper and a drizzle of olive oil. Remove the now-hot baking surfaces from the oven and, working quickly, transfer the pizzas on to them. I find a cake lifter or similar works best for this.

Bake for 10 minutes or until the base has become crisp and the potato is cooked. Serve immediately.

Arguably, this recipe could be in my speedy food chapter, but somehow it felt wrong there. I think this is the sort of soup you should take your time about, stirring it slowly, picking through the clams and generally reducing the pace a bit. Best enjoyed after a long day with a good glass of white.

CLAMS WITH A POTATO AND FENNEL SOUP

SERVES 4–6

2 banana shallots
2 garlic cloves
2 large fennel bulbs, trimmed
450g (1lb) potatoes, peeled
3 tablespoons olive oil
knob of butter
700ml (1¼ pints) chicken or
    vegetable stock
500g (1lb 2oz) fresh clams
250ml (9fl oz) white wine
½ teaspoon Dijon mustard
wee squeeze of lemon juice
salt and freshly ground black pepper

To garnish
chopped chives
Basil Oil (see page 52, optional)
lemon wedges

Chop the shallots, garlic, fennel and potatoes into cubes of roughly the same size.

Heat the oil and butter in a large saucepan over a medium heat, then add the veg. Stir, then cover the pan with a lid and allow the veg to sweat over a medium heat for 10 minutes. Add the stock and cook for a further 20–25 minutes.

Meanwhile, cook the clams. Put them into a large saucepan with the wine and bring to the boil. Cover and cook over a medium heat for 5 minutes or until they have all opened. Discard any that remain shut.

Take the soup off the heat, then stir in the mustard and lemon juice. These additions help to enhance the sweetness of the fennel and will give the soup a nice wee kick. Blitz in a blender or with a stick blender until the soup is silky smooth, then season to taste. Serve in bowls topped with a generous portion of clams, some chives and, if you fancy making it, a drizzle of Basil Oil, with lemon wedges on the side.

During springtime, we get a great load of excellent lamb from our local farmers and friends John Bryce and his son Laurence. The lamb has normally been reared in the field in front of us, to the left of us or a mile up the road from our house "Meikle Logie", hence the title of this recipe. The meat is as local as you can get, and without a doubt this is the best way to eat meat. It is well worth asking your local farmer if they will sell you some meat, or your local butcher if they source locally. Not only will you probably get a cheaper price than you would for cuts of meat that have been flown around the world twice over, but the quality of the meat and the welfare of the animals will be much better. It is good to support the committed farmers close to you, and relying on their products might introduce you to new cuts of meat you wouldn't otherwise try. We enjoy this dish on Easter Sunday, prepped and cooked simply, with lots of garlic and rosemary and a hearty serving of roasted veggies.

MEIKLE LOGIE LAMB

SERVES 6–8

1 leg of lamb, about 2 kg (4lb 8oz)
2 garlic bulbs
large bunch of rosemary
1 lemon, quartered
4 banana shallots, quartered
olive oil
200g (7oz) potatoes
2 red onions
200g (7oz) parsnips
200g (7oz) celeriac
200g (7oz) carrots (preferably coloured)
200ml (⅓ pint) lamb or vegetable stock
200ml (⅓ pint) red wine
1 large leek, roughly chopped
100g (3½oz) French beans, trimmed
200g (7oz) frozen peas
small bunch of fresh mint, leaves picked and chopped
salt and freshly ground black pepper

Prepare the lamb the night before cooking. Put the leg of lamb into a roasting tray, then make lots of small slits across the surface using a sharp knife. Peel the cloves of one of the garlic bulbs and slice them roughly. Stick a slice of garlic into each cut. Break off pieces of rosemary from one-third of the sprigs and also stick these into the cuts. Cover the lamb with clingfilm and refrigerate overnight.

Preheat the oven to 200°C (400°F), Gas Mark 6. Remove the clingfilm from the lamb. Add the remaining rosemary sprigs to the roasting tray. Halve the remaining garlic bulb horizontally and add it to the tray. Squeeze the juice from the lemon quarters over the lamb, then add the squeezed-out pieces of rind to the tray, too. Arrange the quartered shallots around the meat. Drizzle 2 tablespoons of olive oil over the lamb and season with salt and pepper. Roast for 1½ hours.

Remove the tray from the oven (leave the oven switched on), cover the lamb with kitchen foil and then a few tea towels and leave it to rest for at least 30 minutes, although 1 hour is best.

While the meat is resting, prepare the vegetables. Peel then cut the potatoes, onions, parsnips, celeriac and carrots so that they are chopped into pieces of roughly the same size. Place the chopped veggies in a roasting tray, drizzle in about 2 tablespoons of olive oil, season with salt and pepper and toss to coat the vegetables in the oil. Roast for 30 minutes or until the vegetables are almost cooked.

Recipe continued overleaf.

Meanwhile, make the gravy. Drain off the lamb juices from the roasting tray and strain them into a saucepan. Add the stock and wine. Bring the mixture to the boil, then simmer for about 10 minutes until the liquid has reduced by roughly half and has thickened slightly.

Remove the roasting tray with the veggies from the oven once the veggies are nearly cooked, stir in the chopped leek and the French beans so that they get a good coating of oil and roast for a further 10 minutes.

Bring a kettle of water to the boil. Place the peas in a bowl and cover with boiling water. Leave to stand for 2 minutes, then drain. Put the peas into a bowl and stir through the chopped mint.

Place all the vegetables on a big platter. Arrange the lamb and shallots on top. Carve the meat and serve with the gravy.

The best lamb I have ever had was as little harissa-spiked cutlets in Ottolenghi's Islington restaurant in London a few years ago. I had never been wild about lamb prior to this (the one exception to the rule being the Meikle Logie Lamb on page 163), but my dad had always waxed lyrical about the stuff (I learnt early on that the providing of lamb chops was a speedy way to get on his good side). After completely devouring the cutlets on offer at Ottolenghi's, I vowed I would try again with lamb and have been pleasantly surprised by its versatility, particularly when cooked with spices. I have been taking great delight in lamb meatballs packed with loadsa fresh mint, and I wrote a recipe, published in The Scotsman, *for lamb shoulder cooked low and slow with pomegranates. I may not have done Ottolenghi's version justice here, but I give you a very easy recipe that everyone can cook and enjoy at home, lamb lover or not.*

HARISSA-SPICED LAMB CUTLETS

SERVES 4

125g (4½oz) natural yogurt
2 tablespoons harissa
   (paste, not powder – see page 269
   for homemade)
2 garlic cloves, finely chopped
4–8 lamb cutlets

Mix the yogurt, harissa and garlic together in a bowl until combined, then add the lamb cutlets and mix with the flavoured yogurt, ensuring they are well coated. Cover the bowl with clingfilm, then leave to marinate in the refrigerator for at least 2 hours, but preferably overnight.

When ready to cook, heat a griddle pan over a very high heat. When the pan is almost smoking, place the cutlets in the pan and cook for about 2 minutes on each side. You want the lamb to still be pink inside, so don't overcook them. If you are nervous about overcooking them, cook one cutlet to start with, leave it to rest, then cut it open to check it before cooking the rest – it should be blushing. Set aside to rest for at least 10 minutes or more. (During this time you can add any excess marinade to the pan and cook for a few minutes to loosen any sticky lamb pieces left. You could toss this liquid through some plain couscous and add plenty of chopped fresh mint for a delicious accompaniment to the meat.)

My sister Hebe is a year and a half younger than me and painfully cooler and trendier than I will ever be. She is also obsessed with ribs. Once, when we were out for lunch, a waitress recommended she go for a half-size portion of ribs, as she felt the full rack would be too much for Hebe. Of course, this was like a red rag to a bull and Hebe defiantly polished off a full portion, plus extra chips, in a performance that was impressive from any onlooker's point of view. In her honour, I present my version of sticky ribs, a recipe that is (I have been told several times) the best in this book. Ribs are one of those social dishes I enjoy cooking for crowds you love and know well – those that won't mind a big smear of sauce on your cheek or the sticky fingers that get everywhere. I know Hebe wouldn't have it any other way.

HEBE'S STICKY RIBS AND SLAW

SERVES 4
(OR 2 HUNGRY HEBES!)

2kg (4lb 8oz) spare ribs

For the marinade
150g (5½oz) your favourite barbecue
　sauce
50g (1¾oz) tomato ketchup
2 tablespoons soy sauce
2 tablespoons clear honey
2 tablespoons light soft brown sugar
2 tablespoons olive oil

For the coleslaw
50g (1¾oz) mayonnaise
50g (1¾oz) soured cream
juice of ½ lemon
125g (4½oz) white cabbage,
　finely shredded
125g (4½oz) red cabbage,
　finely shredded
125g (4½oz) Savoy cabbage,
　finely shredded
3 spring onions, finely shredded
2 Granny Smith apples,
　finely cut into matchsticks
2 large celery sticks, finely shredded
50g (1¾oz) white poppy seeds,
　toasted (optional)
salt and freshly ground black pepper

In a bowl, stir all the marinade ingredients together until smooth.

Put the ribs into a deep roasting tray and coat them with the marinade. Cover the tray with kitchen foil and leave in the refrigerator to marinate for at least 6 hours, but overnight is best. Remove the ribs from the refrigerator, keeping the kitchen foil covering intact, 1 hour before cooking to bring them up to room temperature.

Preheat the oven to 160°C (325°F), Gas Mark 3.

Once the ribs are up to room temperature, cook for 1½ hours with the kitchen foil still in place. Then whack up the oven temperature to 200°C (400°F), Gas Mark 6, and remove the foil. Cook for a further 30 minutes until the ribs are dark and sticky, with not a huge amount of marinade liquid left in the pan.

Towards the end of the cooking time for the ribs, make the slaw. In a bowl, mix the mayo, soured cream and lemon juice together, then season lightly. Toss through the shredded vegetables until they are well coated. Mix in the toasted poppy seeds, if using. Serve the slaw alongside the ribs.

The best way to enjoy this tasty dish, in my humble opinion, is with the mixture stirred through a big bowl of pappardelle and topped with grated Parmesan and finely chopped parsley. Alternatively, you can go more traditional and serve the casserole with mash and some wilted spinach.

SLOE GIN-BRAISED VENISON

SERVES 4

knob of butter

glug of olive oil

3 banana shallots, finely chopped

3 celery sticks, finely chopped

2 carrots, finely chopped

1 tablespoon juniper berries, crushed (use a pestle and mortar)

2kg (4lb 8oz) boneless venison (shoulder or neck), diced

175ml (6fl oz) sloe gin

vegetable stock, to top up

salt and freshly ground black pepper

To serve

grated Parmesan cheese

fresh chopped flat leaf parsley

Preheat the oven to 150°C (300°F), Gas Mark 2.

Heat the butter and oil in a large casserole dish with a lid over a medium heat and add the veg to the pan. Cook until the shallots begin to become translucent.

Add the juniper berries to the pan with the meat and allow to brown slightly. Cover with the sloe gin and season lightly. Top up with vegetable stock until everything is just covered. Put on the lid, transfer to the oven and braise for 2½–3 hours or until the meat is falling apart and the sauce is well reduced. Serve scattered with grated Parmesan and chopped parsley.

This is one of the first recipes I thought of when I sat down to write this book. It very much embodies the style of eating and cooking I have adopted and wanted to share – a big platter of good, honest, fuss-free food, for relaxed and easy eating. Fillet of beef is an expensive cut, but this big salad doesn't call for a huge amount of it. It does really add to the dish, but you can use less or omit it if you're on a tight budget. Also, I have a flatmate who would eat this beef dish day in, day out and would recommend serving it with nothing else. Feel free to omit the other elements of the dish and simply whack a few slices of the beef in some good bread with plenty of mayo. If it's good enough for Thomas...

BEEF WITH QUINOA, LENTILS, RADISHES AND A PARSLEY DRESSING

⁂

SERVES 6–8

2cm (¾ inch) fresh root ginger, roughly chopped

2 garlic cloves, roughly chopped

1 teaspoon pink peppercorns

1 teaspoon black peppercorns

1 teaspoon salt

1 tablespoon olive oil

500g (1lb 2oz) fillet of beef

150g (5½oz) quinoa (a mix of red and white, if you can get it)

150g (5½oz) Puy lentils

850ml (1½ pints) water

big bunch of flat leaf parsley, leaves picked, stems and half the leaves roughly chopped (reserve the whole leaves to garnish)

100ml (3½fl oz) olive oil, plus extra for the grains

juice of 1 lemon

1 tablespoon white wine vinegar

1 avocado, peeled, stoned and roughly sliced

200g (7oz) radishes, finely sliced

4 spring onions, finely sliced

salt and freshly ground black pepper

Preheat the oven to 200°C (400°F), Gas Mark 6.

Use a pestle and mortar to bash the ginger, garlic, peppercorns and salt together to form a paste. Add the oil and mix again.

Heat an ovenproof frying pan over a high heat until smoking hot. Rub the beef thoroughly with all the ginger paste. Once the pan is hot, place the beef in the pan and cook for 1 minute on all sides, ensuring the outside is completely sealed. Transfer to the oven to roast for 15–17 minutes for medium-rare meat.

While the beef is cooking, weigh out the quinoa and lentils and water into a deep saucepan and bring to the boil. Cook for roughly 20 minutes or until the lentils are soft. The quinoa will be ready at the same time. Drain, then mix in a little olive oil to prevent sticking. Season lightly.

When the beef is cooked, transfer it to a plate, cover the plate with kitchen foil and leave the beef to rest for 15 minutes at least.

For the parsley dressing, put the chopped stems and leaves in a food processor (or in a jug if using a stick blender). Add the oil, lemon juice, vinegar and avocado. Blitz on a high speed until smooth and a vibrant green in colour.

Toss the radishes and spring onions through the quinoa and lentils with the reserved whole parsley leaves.

Finely slice the beef just before serving and lay the slices on a large platter with the quinoa and lentils. Dollop small amounts of the parsley dressing over the salad and serve the remainder on the side for people to help themselves.

Around Bonfire Night and in the depths of winter, perhaps the concept of outdoor eating is a bit of an odd one. (I know plenty of people who think you can only entertain indoors between October and March.) But I adore it, and if wrapped up warm enough with plenty of Mulled Cider (see page 206) on the go, it can be an excellent way to party. Some of my favourite gatherings have happened outside in the bitter cold. I remember one occasion when I was 14 that involved stolen cups of mulled wine, popcorn, glow sticks and very shocking attempts at flirting. Or more recently, when we had fireworks and sparklers over the river at my mum's 50th. Everything looks better with a big fire on a dark night. This recipe follows a chuck-it-in-and-see approach that can be whacked in a low oven for hours and forgotten about. The result is a hearty and warming number that doesn't have to be enjoyed outside, but I would highly recommend it when planning your next party.

TOMATO AND HORSERADISH BEEF
WITH TENDERSTEM BROCCOLI

SERVES 6

2 tablespoons olive oil

2kg (4lb 8oz) beef brisket, rolled and tied

3 red onions, chopped into eighths

3 banana shallots, chopped into eighths

3 bay leaves, bashed

3 garlic cloves, bashed

3 sprigs of rosemary

3 sprigs of thyme

1 teaspoon dried chilli flakes

2 tablespoons jarred horseradish

1 x 400g (14oz) can chopped tomatoes

about 200ml (⅓ pint) boiling water

250ml (9fl oz) red wine

450g (1lb) Charlotte potatoes

300g (10½oz) Tenderstem broccoli, chopped

salt and freshly ground black pepper

Preheat the oven to 140°C (275°F), Gas Mark 1.

In a deep casserole dish, heat the oil over a medium-high heat. Add the brisket and brown on all sides – this should take about 10 minutes.

Add the onions, shallots, garlic and bay leaves to the casserole. Strip the herbs from their stems and add both the leaves and stems to the pan with the chilli. Add the horseradish with the tomatoes, then use the boiling water to swill out the can. Pour in the wine, then stir everything together and season a little. Cover the casserole with the lid, transfer to the oven and braise for at least 10 hours, but longer is fine – simply ensure the liquid doesn't completely dry out.

About 30 minutes before serving, boil the potatoes in a pan of salted water or until cooked. Just before they are cooked, add the broccoli to blanch it.

When the potatoes and broccoli are cooked, drain the veg. The meat should be falling apart and sauce should be thick and rich. Serve in bowls and, if possible, beside a big crackling bonfire.

Pork belly is such a cheap and versatile cut of meat, but it needs to be looked after. I know plenty of people that will avoid it on a menu simply because they have had a badly cooked fatty slab of it years ago. "Low and slow" is the trick with all fattier cuts, and the same applies here. By cooking the meat on top of the apple and onions, they caramelize at a slower rate and make the meat sweeter at the same time. This is perfect for feeding a larger crowd, as it is both time- and cost-effective, and will fill up even the hungriest of guests on a cold, dark winter's night.

SLOW ROAST PORK BELLY
WITH MUSTARD MASH AND ONIONS

SERVES 4–6

2 apples
2 red onions
2 banana shallots or 1 large white
   onion
few sprigs of thyme, leaves picked
1.5kg (3lb 5oz) pork belly
olive oil
700g (1lb 9oz) King Edward potatoes,
   peeled
100ml (3½fl oz) milk
50g (1¾oz) unsalted butter
1 teaspoon Dijon mustard
2 teaspoons grainy mustard
½ teaspoon freshly grated nutmeg
   (or ¼ teaspoon ground nutmeg)
125ml (4fl oz) white wine
1 tablespoon plain flour, if necessary
salt and freshly ground black pepper

Preheat the oven to the highest possible setting.

Core both apples and chop into eighths. Cut the onions into similar-sized wedges. Mix together with the thyme and arrange the mixture in the centre of a roasting tray in a rectangle that's roughly the same size as your pork belly piece.

Score long slashes into the top of the pork belly, leaving a space of 1–2cm (½–¾ inch) between each slash and cutting into the first layer of meat, not any deeper. Season liberally with salt and pepper, then lay the meat on top of the apples and onions. Drizzle with a little olive oil, then roast for 20–25 minutes until the top of the pork belly is crisp and golden.

Reduce the oven temperature to 140°C (275°F), Gas Mark 1, and cook for a further 3–4 hours. Every hour or so, you might want to mix up the onions and apple to prevent any on the outside from burning.

About 30 minutes before the meat is cooked, put the potatoes into a deep saucepan. Cover with water, bring the water to the boil and boil the potatoes for 25–30 minutes, depending on their size, until cooked through. Drain, then add the milk and butter to the pan. Mash roughly, then add the mustards and nutmeg. Stir in well, then season to taste.

Once the meat is cooked, transfer it to a plate to rest in a warm place.

Pour the cooking juices from the roasting tray into a saucepan with the white wine, reserving the apples and onions. Bring to the boil and reduce to the consistency of gravy – you may need to thicken the mixture a little by using the plain flour. Serve the meat with the apples and onions, mustard mash and a generous helping of the gravy.

I was fortunate enough to grow up in the heart of Scotland where we have a bountiful larder. My dad is both a keen shot and fisherman – I spent many evenings when I was wee watching Dad pluck and butcher pheasants, ducks and partridges – and I was taught about the importance of sustainability from a young age. There is a satisfaction, understanding and respect that comes from being involved in the full process – killing, prepping, cooking and eating. The value of the food is emphasized, which is something important that I believe needs to be reintroduced into our culture. All too often, sourcing food involves nothing more than a short trip to the supermarket and an abundance of plastic packaging. I am well aware that not everyone has a dad who can gather game and the likes, but please do be mindful of the original source of your food and, as much as possible, buy high-welfare meat from a trusted supplier.

PARTRIDGE, PANCETTA, PARSNIP

SERVES 2

2–3 parsnips, peeled and roughly chopped
2 partridges, about 800g (1lb 12oz) total weight
small bunch of thyme, leaves picked, stems reserved
50g (1¾oz) salted butter, softened
2 banana shallots or 1 red onion, roughly chopped
2 tablespoons olive oil
2 tablespoons balsamic vinegar
4 slices of pancetta
200ml (⅓ pint) red wine
200ml (⅓ pint) vegetable stock
salt and freshly ground black pepper

Preheat the oven to 200°C (400°F), Gas Mark 6.

Put the parsnips into a saucepan, cover with boiling water and parboil for about 7 minutes or until they begin to soften.

Place the partridges in a deep roasting tray or ovenproof dish with enough room to fit the veg alongside the birds. Sprinkle the thyme leaves over and inside the birds. Put the stems into the tray, too. Rub the skin of both birds with the butter and season. Add the shallots and parsnips, drizzle over the oil and vinegar, then cover the tray or dish with kitchen foil and bake for 30 minutes.

Remove the foil and arrange the pancetta over the top of the birds. Give the veg a wee stir, then return the tray or dish to the oven for 10 minutes to allow everything to crisp up.

Once cooked, remove the birds, put them on a plate and cover them with kitchen foil (leave the bacon in the tray or dish with the veg to prevent it from softening). Leave the birds to rest for at least 15 minutes. Meanwhile, put the veg back in the oven to keep warm.

Just before you're ready to serve, strain the liquid from the veg into a saucepan and add the wine and stock. Bring to the boil and reduce the mixture until it has thickened to a gravy consistency.

Serve the partridge with the crispy pancetta, veg and a good splash of the gravy.

I suppose it is pretty obvious that the only firefighter I know would love all things spicy. I asked him recently what his favourite dishes were and the response was "chillies, chicken, sweet potato and anything you can dream up!" Two out of three ain't bad? Mat, this one is for you, buddy – thank you for the gin and giggles. Sumac is a beautiful spice with a gorgeous lemon undertone that goes so well with chicken. I have added a little chilli to the recipe especially for Mat, but you can keep it child-friendly by omitting this.

SUMAC ROAST CHICKEN
WITH CARROTS AND CHICKPEAS

SERVES 4

400g (14oz) baby carrots left whole
   (or regular carrots, chopped into
   quarters)
1 x 400g (14oz) can chickpeas,
   drained
1 teaspoon ground cumin
2 teaspoons clear honey
olive oil
1 large chicken, about 1.5–2kg/
   3lb 5oz–4lb 8oz
1 garlic bulb, quartered
½ lemon, quartered
reserved rind of ½ juiced lemon
   (see below)
white wine, as necessary
100g (3½oz) whole blanched
   hazelnuts

For the sumac paste

2 tablespoons sumac
½ teaspoon ground cumin
½ teaspoon ground coriander
½ teaspoon dried chilli flakes
juice of ½ large lemon (reserve
   the rind for roasting the chicken
   – see above)
2 tablespoons olive oil
2 garlic cloves, finely chopped
salt and freshly ground black pepper

Preheat the oven to 200°C (400°F), Gas Mark 6.

Begin by making the sumac paste. Using a pestle and mortar, mix all the ingredients except the garlic, including a little salt and pepper until fully combined. Add the chopped garlic and pound it into the paste to break it down further.

In a deep roasting tray (ideally one that can be placed on the table to serve), toss the carrots and chickpeas with the cumin and honey. Drizzle with a little olive oil. Place the chicken, breast side facing upwards, on top of the veg. Add the pieces of garlic bulb to the tray. Place the lemon quarters inside the chicken along with the rind of the juiced lemon half you used to make the sumac paste. Now rub the chicken with the sumac paste, covering the entire surface evenly. At this point, you can cover the chicken with kitchen foil and leave it in the refrigerator for a few hours to marinate, or you can cook it straight away.

Roast the chicken and veg for 1½–2 hours or until the juices from the chicken run clear. Check the chicken after 1 hour, and if it is colouring too quickly, cover it with kitchen foil. At this point, turn the carrots over as well to ensure they become evenly coloured. You can add a little white wine to the tray if things look dry and you feel some extra juice is required.

Once the chicken and veg are cooked through, cover the bird with kitchen foil, then lay a tea towel on top to help keep it warm. Allow to rest for 10 minutes.

While the chicken is resting, roast the hazelnuts quickly in a small frying pan. Once fragrant and slightly golden, chop them roughly.

Serve the chicken with the hazelnuts sprinkled over the carrots, and allow people to spoon a little of the cooking juices over their meat.

It's a worrying state of affairs when we begin to export more produce than we eat ourselves. All too often, we don't make the most of what's on offer where we are right now, instead preferring to import foods from sunnier climates, which by the end of their exhausting journeys, have become a bit bashed and slightly sad-looking. As a cook I am always grateful for the huge amount of options available nowadays, but I do think it is important to bear in mind seasonality and locality. Langoustines are a delicious treat on a hot summer's night, and something Scotland produces a huge quantity of. They are sweeter and tastier than lobster, in my opinion, and are far easier to prepare. Please help to bring back the demand for these wee beauties and read more here: www.scottishlangoustines.co.uk. This recipe makes the most of the sweet flavour of langoustines. When you serve them, make sure you have dipping bowls of water and lemon for people to clean their hands with – it is not a dainty dining experience! Also ensure diners get the delicious meat out of the claws, which can often be forgotten about.

LANGOUSTINES WITH AIOLI

SERVES 4–6

12 fresh langoustines
3 tablespoons olive oil
1 red chilli, deseeded and
  finely chopped
1 banana shallot, finely chopped
2 garlic cloves, finely chopped
splash of white wine
juice of 1 lemon (reserve 2 teaspoons
  for the aioli)
small bunch of flat leaf parsley, leaves
  and stems finely chopped

For the aioli
1 garlic clove, finely chopped
½ teaspoon salt
2 egg yolks
100ml (3½fl oz) good olive oil
2 teaspoons boiling water
2 teaspoons lemon juice (see above)
salt

Place the langoustines in a large pan of cold water. They should be fully submerged. Bring to the boil over a high heat, then simmer for 6–10 minutes, depending on the size of them. Wee ones will not need long.

Heat 1 tablespoon of the oil in a saucepan over a medium heat and cook the chilli, shallot and garlic with the wine for a few minutes – you don't want to colour them, simply soften them slightly to take the edge off a little. Remove the pan from the heat and add the lemon juice (reserving 2 teaspoons for the aioli) and the remaining oil. Stir in the parsley leaves and stems.

Once the langoustines are cooked, drain and coat in the chilli dressing.

To make the aioli, put the chopped garlic in a food processor with the ½ teaspoon of salt, egg yolks and blitz. (Alternatively, put the ingredients into a bowl and use a stick blender to combine them.) Begin to add the oil, a drop at a time, keeping the blender running all the time. You need to be patient at this stage, as adding too much oil too quickly will cause the mixture to split. Halfway through the oil addition, add 1 teaspoon of the boiling water. This helps with the binding of the aioli. Continue to add the oil, stopping a couple of times more to add the remaining teaspoonful of boiling water. Once all the oil has been added, stir in the lemon juice and season to taste. You may want to add a little more garlic if you love it.

Serve the cold langoustines with the aioli.

This is the sort of recipe I think of come the festive season, when everything feels just that little bit more luxurious. Every Christmas, we begin our feast with a variety of beautiful fish, thanks to James and Kilp at East Pier Smokehouse in St Monans, Fife. It was their dazzling beetroot smoked salmon that got me thinking of the different flavours you can infuse salmon with. Nothing says "celebrate" more than tequila, right? Serve this dish with rye crackers, cream cheese and a good squeeze of lime.

TEQUILA GRAVLAX

SERVES 12

750g–1kg (1lb 10oz–2lb 4oz) side of salmon, skin on
300g (10½oz) salt
300g (10½oz) light brown sugar
300g (10½oz) caster sugar
150ml (¼ pint) tequila
finely grated zest and juice of 1 lime
finely grated zest and juice of 1 lemon
1 tablespoon pink peppercorns
1 tablespoon coriander seeds
3 sprigs of fresh dill, leaves and stems roughly chopped
3 sprigs of fresh mint, leaves and stems roughly chopped
3 sprigs of fresh basil, leaves and stems roughly chopped

Rinse the salmon and pat it dry using kitchen paper.

Select a deep-sided tray that fits the salmon snugly in a single layer. Line it with clingfilm in both directions, allowing for a generous overhang on each side of the tray.

Combine the salt and sugars. Sprinkle one-third of the mixture into the tray across the layer of clingfilm, then lay the salmon, skin-side down, on top. Sprinkle half the remaining salt-sugar mixture over the top of the salmon, ensuring the fish is well covered. (Reserve the remaining salt-sugar mixture.) Wrap up the salmon tightly with the overhanging clingfilm. Press another slightly smaller tray on top of the fish and put a few weights, such as some dinner plates or a couple of cans, into this tray. Make sure the weight distribution is as even as possible. Transfer the weighted tray to the refrigerator and leave to cure for 24 hours.

The next day, prepare the wet cure. Put the tequila and citrus zest and juice into a bowl. Bash the pink peppercorns and coriander seeds using a pestle and mortar until the seeds have broken down a bit. Add these to the wet-cure mix. Stir in the roughly chopped herbs well, then mix in the reserved salt-sugar mixture from the previous day.

Remove the salmon from the tray. Re-line the tray, this time using 4–6 layers of clingfilm and again ensuring there is plenty of clingfilm overhanging the tray. Pour the wet-cure mixture into the lined tray. Unwrap the salmon and discard the excess dry cure and any juices. Place the fish into the wet cure and wrap it tightly with the overhanging clingfilm, ensuring you have no leaks. Replace the top tray and weights and return the fish to the refrigerator to cure for a further 24 hours.

Once the curing time is up, check the salmon – it should be firm all over, but not rubbery. If the fish is still quite soft, re-wrap it in the wet cure and return it to the refrigerator for a further 12–24 hours (you can remove the weights this time, however). When the fish is ready, wipe off the cure and discard. Slice the flesh into wafer-thin pieces using a sharp, fine knife.

- MENU -

WANDERING WEEKEND ROAST

BLOODY MARY ** see page 196*

SUMAC ROAST CHICKEN WITH CARROTS
AND CHICKPEAS ** see page 180*

GREENS, QUINOA AND BLACK ONION
SEED SALAD ** see page 71*

SEED AND GRAIN BEER BREAD
WITH WHIPPED BUTTER ** see pages 123*

ORCHARD CRUMBLE ** see page 244*

Clockwise from top left: Sumac roast chicken with carrots and chickpeas; Greens, quinoa and black onion seed salad; Bloody Mary; Seed and grain beer bread with whipped butter.

DRINKS AND OTHER THINGS TO CELEBRATE WITH

There is an abundance of great gin in the UK right now (try Eden Mill gins, Strathearn Distillery gins or Caorunn for beautifully crafted bottles of the stuff). However, the best G&T I have ever had – and I have enjoyed many – was in Barcelona. A huge glass of cardamom perfumed gin, to be precise. I have failed to get back to Spain for more, so I've found a simple way of making my own.

CARDAMOM GIN

MAKES 500ML (18FL OZ)

500ml (18fl oz) gin (a cheaper brand
   is best for taking on the other
   flavours)
2 tablespoons juniper berries
2 tablespoons green cardamom pods
1 teaspoon fennel seeds
1 teaspoon coriander seeds
2 strips of orange peel (avoid
   including the white pith – it's
   very bitter)
few sprigs of mint (optional)

To serve
ice cubes
tonic water, to top up

Mix all the ingredients together in a jug, then transfer the mixture to a sterilized bottle. Leave in a cool, dark place for 3–4 days.

Strain the drink, transfer it to a clean, sterilized bottle and refrigerate until required.

Serve with plenty of ice and tonic.

A Gimlet was Betty Draper's favourite drink in one of my favourite telly series, Mad Men. I watched it at quite an impressionable age and quickly decided that, when I grew up, I would wear a cropped "pant" like Betty, have immaculate blonde curls like Betty and drink Gimlets like Betty. I have succeeded in one of these goals. No prizes for a correct guess.

ELDERFLOWER GIN GIMLET

SERVES 1

plenty of ice cubes
4 tablespoons gin
1 tablespoon elderflower cordial
cava, to top up
1 lime wedge
fresh elderflowers, to garnish
 (optional)

Place a handful of ice cubes in a glass (I like to use an Old Fashioned glass for this). Pour over the gin, then the cordial, and stir. Top up with a little cava. Squeeze in the juice from the lime wedge, then add the rind. Serve with a few fresh elderflowers, if in season.

For a slightly milder version, top up with soda water or elderflower pressé instead of the cava.

Traditionally, Bellinis require no additional sweetness, as the peaches are so perfectly ripe and juicy in sunny Italia. Britain (let alone Scotland) suffers from a slightly different climate, however, so I have suggested using agave nectar to sweeten our slightly sadder peaches that might not be quite as glorious as they are on foreign soils. But by all means, if you are fortunate enough to discover the perfect peach, ignore this suggestion – you lucky thing.

DOUGHNUT PEACH BELLINIS

SERVES 4–6

5 ripe doughnut peaches
2 tablespoons agave nectar
2 tablespoons lemon juice
75cl bottle of Prosecco

Chill your glasses for at least 1 hour before serving. It is traditional to serve Bellinis in small tumblers, but you can, of course, use tall Champagne flutes if you prefer.

In a blender or food processor, blitz the peaches (stones removed, but with their skins on) with the agave nectar and lemon juice. Once smooth, you can strain the mixture if you like. However, I quite like the little pink flecks of skin in the purée. Transfer the mixture to a sterilized bottle and chill in the refrigerator.

To serve, spoon 2 tablespoons of the chilled peach juice into the bottom of each of your glasses. Slowly top up with the Prosecco – it will fizz a lot, so take your time. Keep any unused purée refrigerated until required.

I believe in all the healing properties of a Bloody Mary. Boxing Day would not be the same without at least a few glasses of the stuff. This is my basic recipe for when you are feeling particularly indulgent and fancy making one just for yourself. If you have a crowd in and want to make a big jug, simply multiply the quantities of the ingredients, but add just a little Tabasco and Worcestershire sauce, however, as not everyone likes it so strong. Have bottles of the condiments beside your jug of Bloody Mary and allow people to season their own glasses to taste. I would highly recommend splashing out and going for Big Tom tomato juice – there really is nothing like it!

BLOODY MARY

SERVES 1

4 tablespoons vodka
2 tablespoons sherry
175ml (6fl oz) good tomato juice
few drops of Worcestershire sauce
few drops of Tabasco sauce
squeeze of lemon juice, to taste
ice cubes
plenty of cracked black pepper
celery sticks with leaves, to serve

Place the vodka, sherry, tomato juice, Worcestershire sauce, Tabasco and lemon juice in a cocktail shaker with a few ice cubes. Shake well.

Season with the pepper to taste, and add a little more lemon juice if required.

Pour into a tall glass filled with ice and serve with a few celery sticks.

This pretty drink makes a thirst-quenching and revitalizing alternative to the usual fare for sunsets and picnics.

GREEN TEA MOJITOS

MAKES 1 LARGE JUGFUL

400ml (14fl oz) boiling water
6 green tea bags
small bunch of mint, leaves picked,
    plus extra leaves to garnish
100g (3½oz) caster sugar
75g (2¾oz) demerara sugar
ice cubes
2 limes, sliced
500ml (18fl oz) white rum
approximately 1 litre (1¾ pints)
    soda water

Place the boiling water, tea bags, mint and sugars in a saucepan. Bring to the boil, then slide the pan off the heat and leave to infuse for at least 1 hour but preferably refrigerated overnight. Then strain the syrup, transfer it to a sterilized bottle and refrigerate until required.

Fill a large jug with ice cubes. Add the lime slices, then pour over the rum. Add 250ml (9fl oz) of the syrup and top up with the soda water. Stir in the extra mint leaves. (You should have enough syrup left over to make another jugful.)

As the daughter and granddaughter of huge whisky fans, I was always going to like the stuff, but more often than not, I find myself drinking it neat, tending not to think of it as a cocktail spirit. I was converted by a Whisky Mojito in Manchester after a very long day. It fairly packs a punch. This is a great cocktail all year round, but there is something even more comforting about this come the end of summer, when the sun is setting that wee bit earlier.

WHISKY MOJITOS

SERVES 4

plenty of ice cubes
2 handfuls of mint leaves
50ml (2fl oz) agave nectar
4 teaspoons soft light brown sugar
juice of ½ lemon
approximately 4 double shots
  of whisky
soda water, to top up
lemon slices, to serve

Fill 4 tall glasses with ice. Bash half the mint leaves together with the agave nectar and brown sugar until you have a sort of paste (a pestle and mortar works best for this job). Add the lemon juice and muddle again until you have a sort of syrup.

Strain the mixture and divide it between the 4 glasses. Add a double shot of whisky to each glass. Tear the remaining mint leaves and distribute them evenly between the drinks, saving a few pretty leaves for the tops of the glasses. Finish by topping up the glasses with soda water and adding the last mint leaves. Serve with a few lemon slices in case people want an extra citrus kick.

As someone who leans towards the more bitter style drinks, I am not very enthusiastic about supermarket lemonade. However, this alternative can be so easily customized with citrus and sweetness it is ideal for my palate. The mint is a great addition so I would encourage its appearance regardless of the berry you choose. Enjoy as the ultimate daytime quencher with loads of ice and put your feet up.

ANY BERRY LEMONADE

SERVES 6
(MAKES ROUGHLY 1 LITRE/
1¾ PINTS)

juice of 4 large lemons (you need
  roughly 125–150ml/4–5fl oz)
100g (3½oz) caster sugar
200g (7oz) berries (blackcurrants,
  blueberries, strawberries, cherries
  or raspberries all work well)
small bunch of fresh mint,
  leaves picked
ice cubes
500ml (18fl oz) sparkling water

Put the lemon juice into a saucepan with the caster sugar and a wee splash of cold water. Bring to the boil over a medium heat, stirring regularly. Once the sugar has fully dissolved, remove the pan from the heat. Leave the mixture to cool for 10 minutes.

Transfer the mixture to a blender or food processor with your berries and mint leaves. Blitz on a high speed setting until you have a smooth juice.

Pour the juice over glasses filled with ice until they are one-third to half full, then top up with the sparkling water.

This one is dangerously drinkable, particularly when made during the height of the blood orange season. A glass of sunshine to see you through the last of the winter darkness.

BLOOD ORANGE VODKA BLUSH

MAKES 1 LARGE JUGFUL

250ml (9fl oz) blood orange juice
   (juice of approximately 4–5 oranges)
½ pomegranate
juice of 1 lime
100g (3½oz) caster sugar
plenty of ice cubes
350ml (12fl oz) vodka
700ml–1 litre (1¼–1¾ pints) soda
   water
blood orange slices, to garnish

Pour the orange juice into a saucepan. Squeeze over the pomegranate half to release its juice – the seeds will drop into the pan, but that's nothing to worry about. Add the lime juice and caster sugar. Bring to the boil over a medium heat for a few moments until all the sugar has dissolved. Remove from the heat and strain into a sterilized bottle.

To serve, quarter fill a large jug with ice. Pour over your blood orange juice mixture. Add the vodka and top up with soda water – the quantity will depend on how strong you want the drink to be. Finish with a few slices of blood orange.

We always use ginger beer in Pimm's. I avoid lemonade, as I tend to find it quite sweet – unless you can find a more traditional, sharper-tasting variety. Borage flowers are very easy to grow yourself, but can be found in big supermarkets during the summer, or online.

PIMM'S

MAKES 1 LARGE JUGFUL

plenty of ice cubes
500ml (18fl oz) Pimm's
juice of 1 large orange
300g (10½oz) strawberries, halved
½ cucumber, sliced
big bunch of mint, leaves picked
handful of borage flowers
handful of pansies or any other
   edible flowers
1.5 litres (2¾ pints) ginger beer
   or ginger ale

Fill a large jug with ice cubes. Pour over the Pimm's and orange juice. Add the strawberries and cucumber, as well as the mint and flowers. Top up with the ginger beer.

This recipe was drunk at the bonfire where I had my first kiss.
Surprisingly, I remember the taste of the cider a lot better!

MULLED CIDER

MAKES 1 LARGE PANFUL

1.5 litres (2¾ pints) dry cider
125ml (4fl oz) Calvados
500ml (18fl oz) cloudy apple juice
75g (2¾oz) light brown sugar
rind of 1 orange, cut into thick strips
10 cloves
2 cinnamon sticks, broken in half
5cm (2 inch) chunk of fresh root
  ginger, peeled and roughly sliced
3 star anise

Place all the ingredients in a large saucepan and bring to a slow simmer over a medium heat. Reduce the heat to low and allow to mull for 30–35 minutes.

Serve warm in glasses or mugs.

This is a lovely thing to keep in the fridge during summer for surprise visits from friends and sunny drinks parties. It is a nice option for those that do not drink alcohol, but can also be transformed into a great cocktail with a little vodka and soda water. It is also blissfully easy to make.

LEMON GRASS CORDIAL

MAKES 1 X 750ML (26FL OZ) BOTTLE

575ml (1 pint) water
400g (14oz) caster sugar
5cm (2 inch) piece of fresh root ginger (unpeeled), chopped into small chunks
1 large lemon, thinly sliced
1 large orange, thinly sliced
1 lime, thinly sliced
4 lemon grass sticks, bashed until bruised

Bring the water and sugar to the boil in a deep saucepan over a medium heat. You want all the sugar to dissolve fully, leaving a clear liquid.

Add the ginger and citrus to the sugar syrup along with the lemon grass. Boil for a further 4–5 minutes, then take the pan off the heat and set aside to cool. Cover and leave for 1–2 days to infuse.

Strain the drink and transfer it to a sterilized glass bottle. Keep, refrigerated, for up to 1 month.

South Americans have long been championing this combination of spicy and sweet, and rightly so. I love hot chocolate to be quite rich and bitter, so this recipe relies solely on any sweetness from the chocolate and the cinnamon. But if you are used to a much sweeter affair, add a wee spoonful of sugar, or honey as suggested below. If you are feeling extra indulgent, you could serve the hot chocolate with a dollop of whipped cream, some chocolate shavings and a slice of chilli.

CHILLI HOT CHOCOLATE

SERVES 6–8

700ml (1¼ pints) milk
3 small red chillies, halved, deseeded
    and cut into thirds
3 cinnamon sticks
1 teaspoon vanilla bean paste
200g (7oz) dark chocolate (55–75%
    cocoa solids works best), finely
    chopped
250ml (9fl oz) single cream
tiny pinch of salt
clear honey, to sweeten (optional)

In a large saucepan, heat the milk, chillies, cinnamon sticks and vanilla over a medium heat. Bring to a simmer, then remove the pan from the heat, cover with a lid and leave to stand for 10 minutes to allow the spices to infuse the milk.

Put the chopped chocolate in a bowl. Strain the infused milk on to the chocolate. Stir the mixture, then transfer to the same saucepan in which you heated the milk along with the cream. Heat gently over a medium heat, stirring until well combined. Add the salt, then taste the hot chocolate – if you find the mixture too bitter, add a wee squeeze of honey and taste again to check the sweetness.

I believe spending money on fancy jars of olives is a huge waste. Buy the ones in brine for a fraction of the cost, drain, then dress them up however you wish. They keep fantastically well in the fridge and make for cracking gifts. Chilli and fennel is one of my favourite combinations for dressing olives, but you can substitute the fennel for any spice, really. And by all means, use red chillies or black olives. There are endless possibilities, all of which will save you a fortune. (P.S. These olives make for a pretty special dirty Martini. If you are feeling brave, I am sure they would make an exquisite second one and, arguably, an even better third one…)

FENNEL AND CHILLI OLIVES

MAKES 1 x 450G (1LB) JAR

1 tablespoon fennel seeds
100ml (3½fl oz) olive oil
6 garlic cloves, finely sliced
juice and rind of 1 lemon (use a
   vegetable peeler to cut long,
   thick strips of rind)
1 green chilli, deseeded and sliced
250g (9oz) green olives

In a large frying pan, toast the fennel seeds over a high heat for 2–3 minutes until fragrant.

Reduce the heat to low and add the olive oil. Once the oil is hot but not smoking, add the garlic slivers to the pan. If the pan is too hot, the oil will splutter and the garlic will burn, losing the flavour, so test with one sliver first to ensure the oil is not too hot. The garlic should only give off a little aroma when added, and should not colour quickly. Add the chilli.

Add the lemon rind to the pan with the lemon juice. Mix the garlic, chilli and lemon rind around, ensuring nothing is frying – you are only looking for the oil to be infused. Allow to sit on the heat for 2–3 minutes before adding the olives.

Now add the olives and turn off the heat. Stir to coat the olives with the infused oil, then leave to cool completely.

Spoon the olives into a sterilized jar and pour the oil over the top, then seal. If there is not enough oil to cover the olives, simply top up with a little more olive oil and shake to mix. These olives will keep, refrigerated, for up to 1 month.

A great bar snack that will satisfy the age-old after-work craving for both sweet and salty. The nuts last forever if stored in an airtight tub and can be bagged up and finished with a bow to be given as a dinner party gift.

CANDIED ROSEMARY NUTS

FILLS 2–3 x 450G (1LB) JARS

50g (1¾oz) light brown sugar

50ml (2fl oz) water

½ teaspoon salt

1 teaspoon smoked paprika

1 teaspoon ground cinnamon

½ teaspoon mixed spice

½ teaspoon ground cumin

2–3 large sprigs of rosemary

450g (1lb) mixed nuts (almonds, cashew nuts, hazelnuts and pecan nuts are all good candidates)

Preheat the oven to 180°C (350°F), Gas Mark 4. Line a large baking tray with baking paper.

In a saucepan, gently heat the sugar, water, salt and spices together over a low heat.

Once the sugar has dissolved, strip the rosemary sprigs and add the leaves to the spiced syrup. Add the nuts and stir well to coat them all.

Tip the mixture onto the prepared baking tray and spread the nuts about so that they are not overly clumped together. Bake for 8–10 minutes or until the nuts are no longer sticky. Allow the nuts to cool completely, then transfer to a bowl and serve with a stiff drink.

Here's a quick way of making your own antipasti at home. It can be adapted to include aubergine, onion or any other classic veggies you fancy. I like to griddle the veg, as I reckon it helps maintain a bit of the crunch and gives you a lovely stripy effect that looks very appealing. Serve with good bread to mop up any extra oil. You could also cook a load of couscous and mix the antipasti through it with some olives for a substantial salad or side dish. Any excess oil is great reused in dressings.

SORT OF ANTIPASTI

SERVES 4–6

3 courgettes (a mix of green and
   yellow is great)
3 yellow peppers
small bunch of fresh flat leaf parsley,
   leaves picked and finely chopped
100ml (3½fl oz) good quality extra
   virgin olive oil
pinch of salt
wee squeeze of lemon juice
100g (3½oz) Manchego cheese,
   crumbled (optional)

Heat a griddle pan over a very high heat.

Slice the courgettes on the diagonal to a thickness of roughly 3–4mm (⅛ inch). Core and deseed the pepper, then cut it into chunks that are roughly the same size as the courgette slices.

Once the pan is screaming hot, lay the courgette slices on top and cook for about 1 minute – you are looking for striped char marks, but don't let the slices burn. Repeat on the other side. Remove from the griddle pan and set aside on a plate.

Repeat the chargrilling process with the peppers and any remaining courgettes that didn't fit in the pan first time around.

For the dressing, put the parsley and oil into a bowl and stir well. Add the salt and lemon juice, then the chargrilled veggies and mix to coat them. Crumble in the cheese, if using.

Transfer to a sterilized jar and keep, refrigerated, for up to 1 week.

Sweet or salty? Or spicy? Or all three?! A twist on the classic, this is a tasty last-minute snack that will take you less time to knock up than the adverts before a film.

SPICED POPCORN WITH LIME

SERVES 4–6

splash of sunflower oil
100g (3½oz) popcorn kernels
50g (1¾oz) unsalted butter
1 teaspoon clear honey
½ teaspoon salt
finely grated zest of 2 limes
½ teaspoon smoked paprika
1–2 teaspoons dried chilli flakes

Heat the oil in a large saucepan set over a medium heat. Add the popcorn, ensuring the kernels lay across the base of the pan in a single layer without overcrowding. Cover the pan with a lid and leave to cook, shaking the pan every few minutes. The popcorn should begin to pop after around 5 minutes. Once the popping begins to quieten, take the pan of the heat but keep the lid on.

Melt the butter in a wee saucepan over a medium-low heat and allow it to colour very slightly, but don't let it burn – you are looking for a golden brown. Once the butter is the right colour, add the honey, salt, zest and paprika. Stir to combine.

Pour the butter mixture over the popcorn and toss well to ensure the popcorn is all coated, then sprinkle over the chilli flakes and mix. (Add as much or as few chilli flakes as you would like, but remember, they are pretty hot!)

- MENU -

BONFIRE NIGHT

MULLED CIDER * *see page 206*

CANDIED ROSEMARY NUTS * *see page 216*

FENNEL AND CHILLI OLIVES * *see page 215*

SWEET POTATO AND PARMESAN FRIES * *see page 106*

TOMATO AND HORSERADISH BEEF WITH
TENDERSTEM BROCCOLI * *see page 175*

WARDROBE CAKE * *see page 147*

From left to right: Sweet potato and Parmesan fries; Tomato and horseradish beef with Tenderstem broccoli; Candied rosemary nuts; Fennel and chilli olives; Wardrobe cake.

SWEET PLATES AND PUDS

Roasting fruits is a technique I love when it comes to puddings. It enhances the natural sweetness and the resulting texture is soft and fluffy, which goes wonderfully with any slightly bitter creamy dairy product, yogurt and crème fraîche being my top two choices. This is a great recipe if you have slightly under- or overripe apricots – simply adjust roasting times accordingly. The sorbet will keep well in the freezer for up to 2 months.

YOGURT SORBET AND ROASTED APRICOTS

SERVES 4–6

For the sorbet
250g (9oz) caster sugar
50g (1¾oz) liquid glucose
200ml (⅓ pint) water
1 teaspoon vanilla bean paste
500g (1lb 2oz) natural yogurt

For the apricots
6 apricots, stoned and halved
25g (1oz) unsalted butter
2 tablespoons clear honey
2 teaspoons vanilla bean paste
2 tablespoons golden caster sugar
few sprigs of thyme, leaves picked

To make the sorbet, heat the sugar, glucose and water in a saucepan over a medium-low heat until the sugar has fully dissolved. Take the pan off the heat, add the vanilla and yogurt and whisk together to combine. (If there are any lumps, return the pan to the hob over a gentle heat, but you don't want to overdo it.) Once the mixture is smooth, leave it in the refrigerator to cool for 15 minutes. When cold, churn the mixture in an ice-cream maker following the manufacturer's instructions. Once set, transfer the sorbet to an airtight plastic container and freeze for 3–4 hours before serving.

For the apricots, preheat the oven to 180°C (350°F), Gas Mark 4.

Arrange the apricot halves, with cut sides facing up, in a deep roasting tray. Fleck the butter over the top, then drizzle with the honey and vanilla. Sprinkle the sugar over the top. Add the thyme to the tray, then bake for 15–20 minutes for larger fruits, or 12–15 minutes for smaller or riper fruits. Keep an eye on the apricots, however, as you don't want them to cook so much that they lose their structure.

Divide the warm apricots between 4–6 bowls and serve each with a scoop of the sorbet and juices from the roasting tin.

Subtle and silky, this ice cream has hints of bergamot and smokiness from the tea. Serve it with a sprinkling of shortbread and dried lavender for a speedy yet sophisticated pudding.

EARL GREY ICE CREAM

MAKES ABOUT 700ML (1¼ PINTS)

200ml (⅓ pint) milk
450ml (16fl oz) double cream
50g (1¾oz) light brown sugar
5 Earl Grey tea bags
50g (1¾oz) caster sugar
4 egg yolks
2 teaspoons cornflour

In a deep saucepan, heat the milk, cream, brown sugar and tea bags over a medium-high heat. Once the mixture is just about to boil, take the pan off the heat and cover with a lid. Leave to infuse for 15 minutes.

Whisk the caster sugar, egg yolks and cornflour together in a bowl until smooth. Strain the infused milk on top of the whisked egg yolk mixture. Mix well together, then return the mixture to the pan.

Set the pan on the hob over a medium heat and stir the mixture constantly for 5–10 minutes until it begins to thicken. Once it has noticeably thickened, take the pan off the heat. Press a piece of clingfilm on to the surface of the custard to prevent a skin from forming. Leave to cool completely, then chill in the fridge for at least 1 hour.

When the mixture is cool, transfer it to an ice-cream maker and churn following the manufacturer's instructions until set. Freeze for at least 2 hours before serving. If you do not have an ice-cream maker, simply pour the custard into an airtight tub and put it in the freezer. Give it a good stir every 30 minutes for the first few hours, then whenever you remember, until it is set. This will produce a fine ice cream, but I really would recommend investing in an ice-cream maker if you like ice cream. The texture is far silkier and you can buy them for as little as £30 nowadays.

Brambles, or blackberries, are a favourite of mine. There is something instantly pleasing about these juicy dark berries and I almost never say no to them when they are in season, even the more bitter ones sold with a "great for cooking" sticker. I know I will always manage to find a wee place for them in a breakfast, bake or pud. This recipe came about when I had done exactly that.

BRAMBLE AND CARDAMOM ICE CREAM

MAKES ABOUT 700ML (1¼ PINTS)

1½ teaspoons green cardamom pods
175ml (6fl oz) milk
175ml (6fl oz) double cream
300g (10½oz) blackberries
105g (3¾oz) caster sugar
1 tablespoon water
4 egg yolks
2 teaspoons cornflour

Crush the cardamom pods gently until the black seeds are all loose and slightly bashed. Place the seeds and husks in a saucepan with the milk and cream and bring to the boil over a medium heat. Take the pan off the heat and leave to steep for 15 minutes.

In another saucepan, heat the brambles, 25g (1oz) of the sugar and the 1 tablespoon of water over a medium-low heat. Bring to a gentle boil and cook for 5–7 minutes to allow the fruit mixture to thicken a little, much as you would when making a compote. Take the pan off the heat and leave to cool.

In a bowl, whisk the egg yolks (keep the whites for making meringues, which go particularly well with this ice cream) with the remaining sugar and cornflour. Once the mixture is smooth, pour the lukewarm cream and cardamom mix on top, whisking all the time. Pour the mixture back into the pan and cook over a low heat for 5–10 minutes until thickened. Strain into the bramble sauce in order to remove the cardamom husks. Stir well and leave to cool completely, then chill in the fridge for at least 1 hour.

Once the mixture is fully chilled, pour it into an ice-cream maker and churn following the manufacturer's instructions or until set. Freeze for at least 2 hours before serving. If you do not have an ice cream maker, follow the instructions for churning by hand on page 227.

My sister Hebe is obsessed with watermelon. I have caught her on many occasions marching down streets with a huge watermelon underarm and even, when we were on holiday in France, climbing inside the market display in order to find the largest one. So I've had good reason to find different ways of using watermelon. This is a gloriously refreshing sorbet for the height of summer, and makes for a great cocktail when mixed with a little soda water, loadsa fresh mint and a dash more rum.

WATERMELON SORBET

MAKES ABOUT 700ML (1¼ PINTS)

100g (3½oz) caster sugar
50g (1¾oz) liquid glucose
50ml (2fl oz) water
juice of 1 lime
2 tablespoons white rum (optional)
750g (1lb 10oz) watermelon flesh

Heat the sugar, glucose and the 50ml (2fl oz) water in a saucepan over a medium-low heat until the sugar has fully dissolved. Take the pan off the heat and add the lime juice and rum, if using.

In a blender or food processor, blitz the watermelon until very smooth. Add the sugar syrup and blitz again until smooth. Churn in an ice cream maker following the manufacturer's instructions. Once set, transfer to an airtight plastic container and freeze for 3–4 hours before serving.

Macadamia nuts are quite expensive, so I don't tend to use them very often in my baking. For this cheesecake, however, I don't think anything else will do – they have a softness about them, a rich, buttery taste that is gorgeous with ginger. So in my opinion, this baked cheesecake is well worth splashing out on. If you have never made a baked cheesecake, don't worry if you feel you have taken it out of the oven too early – a wobble in the middle is a good thing! It will set as it cools, I promise.

GINGER AND MACADAMIA NUT CHEESECAKE

SERVES 10–12

For the base
200g (7oz) gingernut biscuits
50g (1¾oz) macadamia nuts
100g (3½oz) unsalted butter, melted,
  plus extra for greasing

For the filling
500g (1lb 2oz) mascarpone cheese
350g (12oz) cream cheese
2 tablespoons cornflour
1 teaspoon ground ginger
100g (3½oz) icing sugar
2 eggs
200ml (⅓ pint) double cream
50ml (2fl oz) ginger syrup (from a jar
  of stem ginger)

For the topping
200ml (⅓ pint) double cream
2 tablespoons icing sugar
200g (7oz) macadamia nuts, toasted
4 pieces of stem ginger, finely
  chopped

Preheat the oven to 160°C (325°F), Gas Mark 3. Grease and line a 20cm (8 inch) round loose-bottomed cake tin.

First, make the base. In a food processor, blitz the biscuits and macadamia nuts until fine. Add the melted butter and blitz again until all the crumbs are coated in the butter. Tip the base mixture into your prepared tin and distribute it evenly across the base. Press it down into the tin firmly using the back of a spoon. Refrigerate the base while you make the filling.

To make the filling, beat the mascarpone, cream cheese, cornflour, ginger and icing sugar together in a large bowl. Once the mixture is very smooth, add the eggs and mix again. Stir in the cream and ginger syrup. Pour the mixture on top of the chilled base.

Bake for 50–60 minutes – you are looking for a light golden colour and the filling to be just about set, with a small wobble in the middle. Turn off the oven, prop open the oven door with a wooden spoon so that it remains ajar, and leave the cheesecake to cool in the oven for 1 hour, then transfer to a wire rack and leave to cool completely. By slowly cooling down the cheesecake in this way, it is less likely to crack or split in the middle. Once cool, chill in the fridge. Remove from the tin when chilled and ready to serve.

Just before serving, softly whip the cream and sugar together, then spread the mixture over the top of the cheesecake. Decorate with the toasted nuts and ginger.

Ice lollies are the ultimate bribe with weenies. I would know, having repeatedly used it as a bedtime incentive. These are a delightful fruity affair that will work even on the adults. I love this sweet and luscious peach and raspberry combo, but you could try using a can of lychees in place of the peaches, and blackcurrant instead of the raspberries for a lovely and slightly sharper ice lolly with a glorious deep purple colour.

PEACH AND RASPBERRY ICE LOLLIES

SERVES 6–8

4 ripe peaches, halved and stoned
100g (3½oz) raspberries
75g (2¾oz) caster sugar
5 tablespoons water
300ml (½ pint) double cream
1 teaspoon vanilla bean paste
50g (1¾oz) clear honey
100g (3½oz) condensed milk

Put the peach halves in a saucepan with the raspberries, sugar and the 5 tablespoons of water and bring to the boil over a medium heat. Cook for around 10 minutes or until the peaches are soft. Then transfer the fruit and syrup to a blender or food processor and blitz until smooth.

In a bowl, whip the cream and vanilla together to form soft peaks. Fold in the honey and condensed milk until well combined – the mixture should thicken without further whipping. Take one-third of the fruit purée and one-third of the cream mixture and stir together in a separate bowl. Divide the remaining cream between your ice lolly moulds, then top with the half-and-half mixture. I find using piping bags helps to minimize mess and keep clean lines between each layer. Finally, finish with the remaining fruit purée, then insert a wooden lolly stick into the middle of each mould. Freeze for at least 6 hours or overnight.

This is a bit of a showy dessert and it does take a wee while to nail the macarons but, oh, is it worth it! Make these posh ice cream sarnies for friends who will appreciate your effort and don't even think about wasting them on those without a sweet tooth. They are a treat like no other. I developed this recipe over six years and I think I have (finally) got it pretty foolproof. The quantities may seem oddly precise, but I promise if you follow them to the letter, everything will turn out rosy.

PISTACHIO MACARON ICE CREAM SARNIES

MAKES 8–10

1 x 500ml (18fl oz) tub of good
   vanilla or pistachio ice cream

For the macarons
50g (1¾oz) ground almonds
30g (1oz) pistachio nuts
120g (4¼oz) icing sugar
60g (2¼oz) egg whites
36g (1¼oz) caster sugar
green food colouring paste

Transfer your ice cream from the freezer to the refrigerator and leave it there for 15 minutes to soften. Meanwhile, line a deep 20cm (8 inch) square baking tin with greaseproof paper. Once the ice cream is spoonable, spoon it into your prepared tin and spread it out until the top surface is level – it should be roughly 4–5cm (1½–2 inches) thick. Put the tin into the freezer.

For the macarons, weigh out the almonds, pistachio nuts and icing sugar into a food processor. Blitz on a high speed until the pistachios are well ground down and you have a fine powder.

In a clean bowl, whisk the egg whites until soft peaks form. Add the caster sugar, then whisk again until glossy and stiff. Use a cocktail stick to add a tiny amount of green food colouring paste to the egg whites and whisk again – you are looking for a pastel shade. Once the colouring has been well incorporated, fold in the nut and icing sugar mix. Do this very gently, as you don't want to overmix. The batter should be lump-free and fall from a spatula in a thick ribbon.

Transfer the mixture to a piping bag. Line a baking sheet with a silicone baking mat. (The silicone is very important – I have experienced issues when using regular baking paper for macarons. You can pick up sheets for just a few quid and they will last forever.)

Pipe rounds of the macaron mixture with a diameter of 5–6cm (2–2½ inches) on to the prepared silicone sheet. Tap the baking sheet on the work surface gently to remove any air bubbles in the macaron rounds and to settle the tops. Set aside to dry out for at least 1 hour until a skin has formed on top

Recipe continued overleaf.

– during a Scottish winter, they require 3 hours! The rate the skin develops will depend on the humidity and heat, so a warm, dry place is best. The rounds are ready to bake when you can touch them without getting sticky fingers.

Preheat the oven to 190°C (375°F), Gas Mark 5.

Once the macarons have formed a skin on top, put them into the oven and immediately reduce the heat to 150°C (300°F), Gas Mark 2. Bake for 10 minutes or until the macarons are well risen and firm to touch. Do not let them colour. If you have multiple trays of macarons, bake them one at a time, reheating the oven to 190°C (375°F), Gas Mark 5 in between each batch and again reducing the oven temperature to 150°C (300°F), Gas Mark 2, once you put the tray into the oven. Allow the macarons to cool down on the tray. Peel the macaron shells off the silicone mat. At this point, the unfilled shells will keep in an airtight container for up to 1 week. (You could also fill them with buttercream or ganache, if you prefer.)

An hour before serving, using a round 5–6cm (2–2½ inch) cookie cutter (or one that matches the size of your macarons), cut out discs from the ice cream. Carefully sandwich the ice cream between 2 macarons. (If you want to, you can half-dip these sandwiches in melted white chocolate for an extra treat!) Store in a plastic container in the freezer until required.

This rich torte is balanced with the sharpness of passion fruit for a cake that can be served throughout the year, bringing a bit of fresh fruit sunshine in the winter and a heady dose of chocolate that never goes out of season.

CHOCOLATE PASSION TORTE

SERVES 8–10

4 eggs, separated

150g (5½oz) caster sugar

150g (5½oz) unsalted butter, plus extra for greasing

150g (5½oz) dark chocolate (minimum 54% cocoa solids), broken into pieces

150g (5½oz) ground almonds

For the cream topping and decoration

200ml (⅓ pint) double cream

2 tablespoons icing sugar

50g (1¾oz) pistachio nuts, roughly chopped

seeds from 3–4 passion fruits

Preheat the oven to 180°C (350°F), Gas Mark 4. Grease and line the base and sides of a 20cm (8 inch) round loose-bottomed cake tin.

Put the egg yolks into a medium-sized mixing bowl and the whites into a stand mixer or large bowl. Add 1 tablespoon of the caster sugar to the whites and the remaining sugar to the yolks. Use an electric whisk to beat the yolks until they are pale and fluffy. Set aside.

Melt the butter in a saucepan over a gentle heat, then add the chocolate. Immediately take the pan off the heat and allow to sit for a few moments without stirring. This helps to prevent the chocolate from seizing (it will split if melted at a temperature that is too high), so I wouldn't skip this step. Once the mixture has cooled a little, stir it to ensure the chocolate has fully melted and the mixture becomes smooth and silky.

Now return to your egg whites. Whisk them in the stand mixer on the highest speed setting possible for about 3 minutes until soft peaks form – they should hold their shape when the whisk attachment is lifted from the bowl.

Stir the cooled chocolate mixture into the whisked yolks. You don't need to fold it as such, but do it with a gentle hand, as you don't want to loose too much air. Once combined, add a few tablespoonfuls of the beaten egg whites in order to loosen the mix. Stir through, then add the chocolate mix, the remaining egg whites and the ground almonds and very, very gently fold everything together – a slotted metal spoon works best for this job. Once smooth and lump-free, pour the mixture into the prepared tin (to minimize air loss, do this from a low height).

Bake for 30–35 minutes or until just set. Allow to cool – the cake will crack and sink a little, but that is nothing to worry about.

Once the cake has cooled, make the topping by whipping the cream with the icing sugar in a bowl until soft peaks form. Spoon the cream over the cake. Sprinkle the chopped nuts and passion fruit seeds all over the cream and cake, then serve.

This recipe is for James, a very intelligent man who once said I make excellent "pancettas" when referring to this recipe. It made me smile a lot. Panna cottas are a perfect dessert when it comes to hosting. You can knock them together up to two days in advance and simply store, covered, in the fridge. The bay leaf is optional here, but I love the musky flavour it adds to the sweetness of the white chocolate. You could also try rosemary to achieve this savoury note – simply use 3–4 sprigs and follow the same infusing method as you would with the bay leaves.

WHITE CHOCOLATE AND BAY LEAF PANNA COTTA

MAKES 6

4 gelatine leaves
600ml (20fl oz) double cream
200ml (⅓ pint) milk
75g (2¾oz) icing sugar
1 teaspoon vanilla bean paste
6 dried bay leaves
150g (5½oz) good-quality white chocolate, broken into pieces, plus extra curls for decoration

Soak the gelatine leaves in cold water and set aside to soften.

In a large saucepan, bring the cream, milk, sugar, vanilla and bay leaves to the boil. Watch the mixture, though, as you don't want it to boil over. Once boiling, slide the pan off the heat and allow the mixture to cool for 15 minutes.

Squeeze out any excess water from the now-wrinkled gelatine and stir it into the warm cream until fully dissolved. Add the white chocolate and allow to sit for 5 minutes – don't be tempted to stir the mixture yet in case the chocolate seizes and splits. After 5 minutes, slowly stir the cream mixture until smooth and the chocolate is fully melted. Remove the bay leaves, then pour the mixture into 6 ramekins, small glasses, espresso cups or any other wee dishes you have. Allow to set in the refrigerator overnight before serving decorated with chocolate curls.

*A light and refreshing summer tart that is guaranteed to be
a crowd-pleaser. The bright, white filling topped with glorious
pink pomegranate jewels is a great way to finish an alfresco
feast or to have with a pot of tea with friends.*

POMEGRANATE MILK TART

SERVES 8–10

For the pastry
100g (3½oz) chilled unsalted butter,
 cubed, plus extra for greasing
160g (5¾oz) plain flour, plus extra for
 dusting
15g (½oz) cornflour
50g (1¾oz) icing sugar
2 tablespoons milk

For the filling and topping
4 gelatine leaves
350ml (12fl oz) milk
350ml (12fl oz) double cream
50g (1¾oz) caster sugar
2 teaspoons vanilla bean paste
2 pomegranates

Preheat the oven to 200°C (400°F), Gas Mark 6. Grease a 20cm (8 inch) round, deep fluted loose-bottomed tart tin.

To make the pastry, put all the ingredients except the milk in a food processor and blitz together, then add the milk gradually as you continue to blitz to bring the dough together. Alternatively, rub the butter into the flour, sugar and cornflour until the mixture resembles breadcrumbs, then mix in the milk at the end to bind the dough. Put the dough in a bowl, cover the bowl with clingfilm and chill in the fridge for at least 20 minutes.

Now make the filling. First, put the gelatine leaves in cold water to soften. Heat the milk, cream, sugar and vanilla in a saucepan over a medium heat until just about to boil. Slide the pan off the heat and allow the mixture to cool for 5 minutes or until there is no steam visible.

Drain the gelatine leaves, squeeze out any excess water, then whisk them into the milk mixture.

Roll out the chilled pastry and use it to line the prepared tart tin. Trim off any pastry that overhangs the edges of the tin. Line the pastry with some kitchen foil and cover the base with baking beans. Blind bake (part bake) for 10–15 minutes or until the pastry is pale gold in colour. Remove the baking beans and kitchen foil and return the tart tin to the oven for about another 5 minutes until the pastry is fully baked and golden in colour. Allow to cool completely.

Pour the milk filling into the tart case, then refrigerate for at least 2 hours to allow the filling to set.

Cut the pomegranates in half and squeeze the juice of one of them over the tart. Deseed the remaining pomegranate carefully, then scatter the seeds all over the tart. Serve immediately.

My first taste of sugar was at the age of three. We were staying at my auntie's in the Scottish borders and it was at the height of summer. After a day at the beach we feasted on lots of delicious dishes, but for me, pudding was the highlight. My Auntie Moira produced a mound of meringues similar in size and appearance to Everest. I don't remember much post-meringue, but I am told I ate two, went into a sugar slump very quickly and then slept for hours. I do remember how delicious they were, though. You can top your pavlova with any fruit you fancy, from berries and peaches, to plums and mangoes – meringue is an ivory-coloured canvas.

REDCURRANT PAVLOVA

SERVES 4–6

For the meringue
4 egg whites
280g (10oz) caster sugar
1 teaspoon vanilla bean paste

For the curd
150g (5½oz) redcurrants
2 tablespoons orange juice
4 egg yolks
100g (3½oz) caster sugar
100g (3½oz) unsalted butter

For the cream topping and decoration
300ml (½ pint) double cream
1 teaspoon vanilla bean paste
2 tablespoons icing sugar
300g (10½oz) redcurrants
3 white peaches, stoned and sliced

Preheat the oven to 140°C (275°F), Gas Mark 1. Line a baking sheet with baking paper.

Put the egg whites into the bowl of a stand mixer and whisk on a high speed for 3–4 minutes until soft peaks form. Reduce the speed to medium and add the caster sugar 1 dessertspoonful at a time. Ensure each spoonful is fully incorporated before adding the next. Once all the sugar has been added and the mix becomes thick and glossy, add the vanilla. Test the mixture to see if it is ready by rubbing a small amount between 2 fingers – you should not be able to feel any sugar crystals.

Spoon the meringue on to the prepared baking sheet in a big mound. Shape it into a circle about 23 cm (9 inches) in diameter and 10cm (4 inches) deep. Bake for roughly 2½ hours.

Meanwhile, make the curd. Put the redcurrants in a saucepan with the orange juice and cook over a medium heat for about 5 minutes until they become mushy. Push the berry mixture through a sieve to remove any skin or seeds.

Whisk the egg yolks and sugar together in a bowl until light and fluffy.

Melt the butter in a small saucepan over a low heat, then pour it over the egg mix, stirring constantly. Add the berry juice and mix well. Pour the mixture into a saucepan and cook over a low heat for about 10–15 minutes, stirring constantly to avoid scrambling the egg. It should thicken to a custard-like consistency. Take the pan off the heat and leave the mixture to cool.

Once your meringue is done (it should sound hollow when tapped, but still be slightly soft in the middle), leave it to cool completely. Then transfer it on to a serving plate.

To make the cream topping, whip the cream, vanilla and sugar in a bowl until soft peaks form. Spread the now-cooled curd over the meringue, pushing it just to the edges. Top with the cream and spread it evenly across the top surface of the meringue. Some of the curd will drip down the sides of the meringue, but that's nothing to worry about. Finish with a pretty scattering of the redcurrants and the peach slices and serve immediately.

You cannae beat a crumble. This version is topped with crunchy oats and hazelnuts – which is exactly how it should be if you ask me.

ORCHARD CRUMBLE

SERVES 6–8

125g (4½oz) caster sugar
100ml (3½fl oz) water
wee squeeze of lemon juice
1 teaspoon ground cinnamon
½ teaspoon ground ginger
½ teaspoon ground nutmeg
300g (10½oz) apples, cored and cut
    into 8 wedges
300g (10½oz) pears, cored and cut
    into 8 wedges
300g (10½oz) quince (or more apples
    and pears if you can't source them),
    cored and cut into 16 wedges
custard or crème fraîche, to serve
    (optional)

For the crumble topping
100g (3½oz) rolled oats
100g (3½oz) spelt flour (white or
    wholemeal)
100g (3½oz) unsalted butter, grated
    or finely sliced
50g (1¾oz) demerara sugar,
    plus extra for sprinkling
100g (3½oz) whole blanched
    hazelnuts, roughly chopped

Preheat the oven to 180°C (350°F), Gas Mark 4.

Heat the sugar, water, lemon juice and spices in a pan (I like to use a round, shallow cast-iron pan that can be used on the hob, in the oven and to serve) over a medium heat until the sugar has dissolved. Add all the fruit and cook for 5–7 minutes or until the fruit has softened and begins to turn golden in colour. Set aside.

For the crumble, weigh out the oats and flour into a bowl. Add the butter and sugar. Rub together using your fingertips until the mixture resembles fine breadcrumbs. Stir half the chopped nuts into the mix.

If you have cooked the fruit in an ovenproof pan, shake the dish so that the fruit lays evenly across the base, then sprinkle the crumble mixture over the top. Finish with a little more sugar and the remaining hazelnuts. If you haven't cooked the fruit in your serving dish, simply transfer it to a shallow ovenproof dish, ensuring you get all the delicious cooking juices. If you want to make individual crumbles, divide the fruit between generous-sized ramekins or wee ovenproof dishes. Top as above. At this point, you can keep the crumble refrigerated for up to 4 hours until you are ready to cook.

Bake for 20–25 minutes (15 minutes if you are making individual portions) until golden. Serve immediately with custard or a generous dollop of crème fraîche, if you need a big cuddle.

For several years when I was wee, my mum would make two puddings whenever we were invited to parties. This was not entirely her choice (although I am sure she enjoyed the familiar habit of it all) – her puddings were legendary and so a couple of favourites were often requested. Her pine nut tart was my favourite, and even now, I can still remember the smell of sticky honey and roasted nuts wafting through the house. Back when Mum was knocking this tart up at a steady rate, pine nuts were far cheaper than they are today, so I'll understand if you want to substitute half the quantity of pine nuts with something less expensive, such as flaked almonds, which work well in this recipe.

HONEY AND PINE NUT TART

SERVES 10–12

For the pastry
100g (3½oz) cold unsalted butter, cubed
160g (5¾oz) plain flour, plus extra for dusting
15g (½oz) cornflour
50g (1¾oz) icing sugar, plus extra for dusting
2 tablespoons milk

For the filling
275g (9¾oz) pine nuts
250g (9oz) unsalted butter
200g (7oz) caster sugar
50g (1¾oz) soft light brown sugar
3 eggs
75g (2¾oz) clear honey
75g (2¾oz) plain flour
50g (1¾oz) plain wholemeal flour
1 teaspoon finely grated orange zest (optional)

clotted cream, to serve (see page 279)

Preheat the oven to 170°C (340°F), Gas Mark 3½.

To make the pastry, combine the ingredients in a food processor and blitz until you have a smooth dough. Alternatively, work the butter into the combined flours and sugar using a wooden spoon, then mix in the milk and gently knead until you have a smooth dough. Cover the dough with clingfilm and chill in the refrigerator for 15 minutes.

Meanwhile, for the filling, scatter 225g (8oz) of the pine nuts on a baking tray and toast them in the oven – watch them like a hawk, as they will only take a minute. (If you are substituting almonds for half the pine nuts, toast these along with the pine nuts). Set aside the toasted pine nuts to cool. (Leave the oven switched on.)

Beat the butter and sugars together until light and fluffy, preferably in a free-standing mixer set to a medium speed. Add the eggs, honey and flours and mix again. Once combined, fold in the toasted pine nuts and orange zest, if using, with a wooden spoon or spatula.

Dust your work surface with flour, then roll out the chilled pastry to a thickness of 2–3mm (¹⁄₁₆–⅛ inch). Transfer the pastry to a 23cm (9 inch) round loose-based tart tin and press it gently into the sides. Trim off any excess pastry. Spoon the filling into the tart case and spread until the surface is level. Sprinkle the remaining pine nuts on top and bake for 35–40 minutes. Dust with icing sugar and serve with clotted cream.

I love the flavour of chestnuts and every year, come the festive season, I begin plotting all the different dishes in which I intend to include them. Chestnut flour is such an expensive product to get hold of, so my alternative way of using chestnuts is a much cheaper method of capturing their richness in a bake. For this tart I use cooked vacuum-packed chestnuts that are available in most supermarkets, but if the mood takes you and carols are playing, you can go to the bother of roasting and peeling chestnuts yourself. Serve each slice of this tart with a big dollop of crème fraîche.

CHESTNUT AND PEAR FRANGIPANE

SERVES 8–10

For the pastry

100g (3½oz) cold unsalted butter, cubed

175g (6oz) plain flour, plus extra for dusting

2 teaspoons cornflour

75g (2¾oz) icing sugar, plus extra for dusting

splash of milk

For the frangipane

150g (5½oz) cooked and peeled chestnuts (the vacuum-packed ones work well), finely grated

100g (3½oz) ground almonds

100g (3½oz) unsalted butter, softened

100g (3½oz) caster sugar

2 eggs

½ teaspoon baking powder

1 teaspoon vanilla bean paste

2–3 large pears, cored and finely sliced

Preheat the oven to 170°C (340°F), Gas Mark 3½.

To make the pastry, blitz the butter, flours and sugar in a food processor, then add the milk at the end to bring the dough together. Alternatively, rub the butter into the combined flours and sugar until it resembles breadcrumbs, then add the milk at the end to bind it. Wrap the dough in clingfilm and chill in the refrigerator for at least 20 minutes.

While the dough chills, make the filling. Put the grated chestnuts in a bowl with the almonds, butter and sugar. Mix well until you have a paste-like batter, then add the eggs, baking powder and vanilla bean paste. Beat again until the mixture is smooth. (You can add a few tablespoons of booze such as brandy or Marsala if you like at this stage.)

To assemble the tart, roll out the chilled pastry on a lightly floured work surface until it is roughly 3mm (⅛ inch) thick. Use it to line a 35 x 12cm (14 x 4½ inch) rectangular tart tin or a 20cm (8 inch) fluted loose-based tart tin. Press the dough into the sides of the tin thoroughly, then trim off any overhanging pastry.

Place the filling into the pastry case and spread it across the base until it fills the case and the surface is smooth all over. Fan the pear slices over the top. Bake for 45–50 minutes or until the chestnut filling is cooked through (it will no longer be soggy to touch). Finish with a dusting of icing sugar.

- GREAT IDEAS FOR -
GIFTS

CARDAMOM GIN * *see page 193*

SPICED TOMATO CHUTNEY * *see page 267*

NUT AND SEED SAVOURY BISCOTTI * *see page 120*

COCOA NIB BROWNIES * *see page 140*

PRESERVED LEMONS * *see page 271*

CIDER-PICKLED CUCUMBERS * *see page 272*

Clockwise from bottom left: Cocoa nib brownies;
Preserved lemons; Cider-pickled cucumbers;
Cardamom gin; Nut and seed savoury biscotti.

ESSENTIALS

A NOTE ON PRESERVING

I got heavily into preserving four or five years ago. (I even won first place for my Tomato and Chilli Jam in 2014 – thank you to the Dunkeld & Birnam Horticultural Society!). It's the process and seasonality I particularly fell for: hours carefully spent prepping fruit at the end of summer, peeling apples for chutney in autumn and stocking up on all the colourful citrus at midwinter. Then you stand and slowly stir a big bubbling mass of amber, golden, deep purple, pink or even green liquid, waiting for the magic to happen. It is a deeply therapeutic process for me and often occurs late into the night with a good playlist on the go.

Preserving is such an important skill when it comes to avoiding food waste. And homemade preserves contain no nasty additives, chemicals or excessive sugar, which are all used in order to reduce costs when mass-producing preserves.

Preserving is a beautifully adaptable craft. Once you get a feel for the various types of set you are after, it is blissfully easy to make any jam recipe your own. I love to add dried flowers, such as rose petals, chamomile or even lavender to batches (lavender works particularly well with peaches or apricots). Fruits can be swapped and doubled up on, depending on what you have a glut of. And homemade preserves make perfect gifts – who wouldn't want little jars of jewel-like jams, beautifully presented and labelled? (But do remember to keep some back for yourself!) You would be mad not to join in and get the sugar thermometer out.

For those very keen to learn more, I can highly recommend Diana Henry's *Salt Sugar Smoke* and Kylee Newton's *The Modern Preserver* – these are both modern-day bibles on the subject.

STEM GINGER CURD

MAKES 1 x 450G (1LB) JAR

100g (3½oz) caster sugar
50g (1¾oz) ginger syrup (from a jar
   of stem ginger)
3 eggs
4 large pieces of stem ginger, finely
   grated
150g (5½oz) unsalted butter

In a bowl, whisk the sugar, syrup and eggs together. Stir in the grated stem ginger.

Put the butter into a large saucepan and melt it over a low heat. Whisk in the egg mixture, then continue to stir for 5–10 minutes. Ensure you keep the heat at a low setting to avoid the eggs scrambling. Once the mixture begins to thicken and coats the back of a wooden spoon, take the pan off the heat. Don't worry if it isn't very thick – it will set as it cools. Pour the curd into a sterilized jar and seal. Store in the refrigerator or up to 1 month.

STRAWBERRY AND ELDERFLOWER JAM

❋

MAKES 4 x 450G (1LB) JARS

1 kg (2lb 4oz) strawberries (if you
    can get wild ones, even better!)
juice of 2 lemons
150ml (¼ pint) elderflower pressé
    (or water)
10 fresh heads of elderflower
750g (1lb 10oz) jam sugar

If the strawberries are large, halve them. Put them into a deep saucepan with the lemon juice and elderflower pressé, bring to the boil and cook for about 10 minutes over a medium heat until the berries have softened.

Add the elderflower heads to the pan and stir through, then add the sugar. Bring to the boil and cook until the temperature of the mixture reaches 104.5°C (220.1°F) on a sugar thermometer, stirring regularly to ensure the mixture doesn't burn at the base of the pan. Once the mixture is up to temperature, take the pan off the heat and, using a sterilized teaspoon, place a little of the jam on a clean, chilled plate. Leave it to cool for a minute or so, then push your finger through the mixture. If it has formed a skin on the surface that wrinkles when pushed by your finger, then it has reached the setting point and the jam is ready. (If the mixture fails the wrinkle test, return the pan to the heat and repeat the wrinkle test again after a few more minutes of cooking.)

Once the jam has reached the setting point, remove and discard the elderflower heads (lots of flowers will have fallen off by then, which is fine, but you want to ensure all the stems are removed). Allow to stand for 5 minutes, then transfer the jam to sterilized jars and seal. Store at room temperature for up to 2 months. Once opened, store in the refrigerator and eat within 4 weeks.

This recipe is for you, Daddy – it is not your mother's (Granny Iso makes legendary marmalade), but it won't kill you to try it.

CLEMENTINE AND VANILLA MARMALADE

MAKES 4 x 450G (1LB) JARS

750g (1lb 10oz) clementines, halved,
    then sliced into fine slivers
juice of 1 lemon
1–1.5 litres (1¾–2¾ pints) water
2 vanilla pods, split lengthways
1kg (2lb 4oz) jam sugar
50ml (2fl oz) whisky (optional)

Discard any clementine pips, then put the slices into a large saucepan. Add the lemon juice, 1 litre (1¾ pints) of the water and the vanilla pods. Bring to the boil, then cook for 20 minutes over a medium-high heat. Add more of the water if it looks as though a lot has evaporated.

Once the clementine rind is soft, add the sugar and whisky, if using. Boil until the temperature of the mixture reaches 105°C (221°F) on a sugar thermometer. Stir frequently and keep an eye on the marmalade, as you don't want it to burn on the base of the pan. Once the mixture is up to temperature, take the pan off the heat and, using a sterilized teaspoon, place a little of the marmalade on a clean, chilled plate. Leave it to cool for a minute or so, then push your finger through the mixture. If it has formed a skin on the surface that wrinkles when pushed by your finger, then it has reached the setting point and the marmalade is ready. (If the mixture fails the wrinkle test, return the pan to the heat and repeat the wrinkle test again after a few more minutes of cooking.)

Allow the marmalade to sit off the heat for 5 minutes, then ladle it into sterilized jars and seal. Store at room temperature for up to 2 months. Once opened, store in the refrigerator and eat within 4 weeks.

Both this and the Rhubarb and Honey Compote on page 264 are unbelievably easy to knock up and will keep, refrigerated, fairly well. Use older, softer fruits to avoid them going to waste. Serve the compotes on top of porridge, waffles or pancakes (see pages 29–31 and 39), with ice cream for a speedy dessert or simply with a dollop of yogurt and a steaming hot cup of tea.

SPICED PLUM COMPOTE

MAKES 2 x 450G (1LB) JARS

400g (14oz) plums, stoned and sliced
   into rough segments
100g (3½oz) blackberries
50g (1¾oz) soft light brown sugar
50ml (2fl oz) orange juice
1 cinnamon stick
5 star anise

Put all the ingredients into a large saucepan, bring to a gentle boil over a medium heat and cook for about 10–15 minutes until the plums are softened and the compote smells fragrant.

Remove the pan from the heat and allow the compote to cool completely, then remove and discard the cinnamon and star anise. Transfer to sterilized glass jars or a clean plastic tub and seal. Store in the refrigerator for up to 2 weeks.

Not having a rhubarb plant in our garden, I become giddy when gifted with these pink stalks, all tied up in a big bundle. The tart, pink fruit makes for a perfect compote when cooked with just a little sweetness provided by the honey. You could also stir through some elderflower cordial once cooked for a summery note. Serve with yoghurt and a good granola (see page 26 for my Fig and Pumpkin Seed Granola) for a perfectly pink breakkie.

RHUBARB AND HONEY COMPOTE

MAKES 2 x 450G (1LB) JARS

5–7 sticks of rhubarb, cut into 3cm (1¾ inch) chunks
50g (1¾oz) clear honey
50ml (2fl oz) orange juice
1 teaspoon vanilla bean paste
1 teaspoon grenadine syrup (optional)

Put all the ingredients into a large saucepan. Bring to a gentle boil over a medium heat and cook for about 5–10 minutes until the rhubarb is soft but still holds some of its shape. Be careful not to overcook it, or it will lose its gorgeous pink colour.

Remove the pan from the heat and allow the compote to cool completely. Transfer to sterilized glass jars or a clean plastic tub and seal. Store in the refrigerator for up to 2 weeks.

I'm a big fan of a cheese board and I like nothing more than to get stuck in to a nice dolly mixture of biscuits, a really good slab of my favourite Cheddar and a wee dollop of this piccalilli on top (see photograph on page 266). This is a great recipe to have up your sleeve when your fridge is groaning with veggies and you need a day of stirring and bottling. Perfect for gifting, however I won't judge you for a minute if you polish off the lot yourself.

PICCALILLI

MAKES 2 x 450G (1LB) JARS

600g (1lb 5oz) mixed veg (include at least 4 of the following: broccoli, cauliflower, Romanesco cauliflower, cucumber, shallots, red and yellow peppers, carrots, peas), chopped into rough 3cm (1¼ inch) chunks

1 tablespoon salt

splash of olive oil

1 tablespoon yellow mustard seeds

1 teaspoon coriander seeds

1 teaspoon cumin seeds

1 teaspoon ground turmeric

1 teaspoon English mustard powder

1 tablespoon plain flour

50ml (2fl oz) water

1 apple, cored and grated

250ml (9fl oz) white wine vinegar

50g (1¾oz) caster sugar

2 tablespoons clear honey

Put the vegetables into a large bowl and sprinkle over the salt. Add enough cold water to just cover the veg, then set aside in a cool place for 1 hour.

Select a large saucepan that's big enough to fit in all the veg. Add the oil and heat it over a high heat. When the oil is hot, add the mustard seeds, coriander seeds and cumin seeds and fry for 1 minute, then reduce the heat to medium and add the turmeric, mustard powder, flour and the water. Stir or whisk well to form a thick paste.

Add the grated apple to the pan, then the vinegar, sugar and honey. Allow the mixture to simmer for 10 minutes until the mixture has thickened a little.

Thoroughly drain the soaking vegetables, then add them to the saucepan. Mix well, then cook for 5 minutes or until the veg are just beginning to soften and the sauce has loosened slightly.

Transfer the mixture to sterilized jars and seal. Store in a cool, dark place for 1 month before opening. If unopened, the piccalilli will keep for 6 months. Once opened, store in the refrigerator and consume within 1 month.

Before Christmas I tend to go on a spice spree. For some reason, it feels like the time of year to load up the store cupboards. I buy lots of little jars and packets, thinking we have run out and need to stock up for the winter. When I return home, however, I always find multiple packets from last year's extravagance – mustard seeds, sesame seeds, coriander seeds and cumin all lying opened and in a very sad state. This often brings chutney to mind, and we end up giving out jars of the stuff as pressies. This is a warming recipe and is particularly delicious in the middle of winter when everyone needs heating up. The chutney is best enjoyed a month after making, but if you are impatient, you can, of course, dive straight in. (The spice cupboard continues to go through stages of both bounty and neglect, by the way.)

SPICED TOMATO CHUTNEY

MAKES 4 x 450G (1LB) JARS

1 large white onion or 3 banana
   shallots, finely chopped
splash of olive oil
300g (10½oz) dessert or cooking
   apples, cored and finely chopped
700g (1lb 9oz) mixed tomatoes (a
   dolly mixture of cherry and beef
   tomatoes is best), finely chopped
5 small red chillies, deseeded and
   finely chopped
5–7 large garlic cloves, minced
3 tablespoons black sesame seeds
150g (5½oz) soft light brown sugar
2 teaspoons salt
1 teaspoon yellow mustard seeds
1 teaspoon ground cumin
1 teaspoon coriander seeds
300ml (½ pint) cider vinegar

Put the chopped onion into a large saucepan with the oil. Set the pan over a low heat, cover it with the pan lid and sweat the onion gently for 5–7 minutes.

Add the apples, tomatoes, chillies and garlic to the pan once the onion is translucent and turn up the heat to medium. Cook for 5 minutes to break down the apples and tomatoes.

Now add the remaining ingredients to the pan and stir well. Bring the mixture to a simmer and cook over a medium heat for 25–30 minutes, stirring intermittently to stop the mixture burning at the base of the pan. Check the consistency of the mixture once the cooking time has elapsed – it should be thickened and almost syrupy.

Take the pan off the heat and leave the mixture to cool for 10 minutes. Pour into sterilized jars and seal. Store in a cool, dark place for up to 6 months, if you don't tuck in immediately. Once opened, keep refrigerated and consume within 4 weeks.

Unlike shop-bought mayonnaise there is a silky luxury about the homemade stuff. It's indulgent, delicious and far easier to make than it is made out to be. Squash some slow-roasted garlic through the mayo for a sweet and slightly smoky alternative. Delicious with the Sweet Potato and Parmesan Fries on page 106.

MAYO

MAKES 1 x 450G (1LB) JAR

3 egg yolks
1 teaspoon Dijon mustard
300ml (½ pint) vegetable oil (or use
    olive oil for a luxurious mayo)
1 teaspoon white wine vinegar
salt and freshly ground black pepper
lemon juice, to taste (optional)

In a food processor, blitz the yolks and mustard until thick and smooth. With the motor still running, slowly pour in the oil in a steady stream. The mixture should be thick and creamy. (If it splits, remove half the mixture, add another yolk and blitz again for a few moments to bring it together. Then add the remaining curdled mixture, but do so very slowly, to avoid the mixture separating again.)

Blitz in the white wine vinegar, then season to taste. You can also blitz in a little lemon juice for a looser consistency, if desired.

Transfer the mixture to a clean plastic tub or a sterilized jar. Store in the refrigerator for up to 1 week.

Harissa was a very trendy ingredient a few years ago, to the point where there was no escaping the stuff. Unfortunately living where I do and with the limited ranges on offer in supermarkets, I had to improvise. This is my preferred version, with not too much chilli heat, but lots of smokier spices and a very rich pepper and tomato base. I don't use rose petals or water as I find it too overwhelming, but if it is to your taste feel free to add a very, very small amount, tasting as you go. This is great swirled into some cool yogurt to make a delicious dip.

HARISSA

MAKES 1 x 450G (1LB) JAR

2 teaspoons coriander seeds

2 teaspoons fennel seeds

2 teaspoons cumin seeds

olive oil

5 garlic cloves, finely sliced

2 banana shallots, finely chopped

1 red pepper, cored, deseeded and finely chopped

2 plum tomatoes, finely chopped

2 red chillies, deseeded and finely sliced

Put the seeds into a large frying pan set over a high heat and toast them for 2–3 minutes until fragrant. Stir them regularly to prevent burning. Put the toasted seeds into a mortar and grind them down to a fine powder using the pestle.

Add a good glug of olive oil and the garlic slices to the same frying pan you used to toast the seeds. Cook gently over a medium heat for about 3 minutes until the garlic has softened.

Add the chopped shallots, pepper and tomatoes to the pan and cook for 10 minutes until slightly reduced. Add the sliced chillies and continue to cook over a medium heat for 10–15 minutes or until the liquid has noticeably reduced and is deep red in colour. Add the ground spices and cook for a final 2 minutes.

Transfer the mixture to a food processor and blitz (alternatively, transfer it to a jug or saucepan and use a stick blender) – it doesn't need to be silky smooth. In fact, a bit of texture is nice. Serve hot or cold. The harissa will keep in a sterilized jar, covered in a layer of oil, in the refrigerator for up to 2 weeks.

I like to put preserved lemons into small jars, using one lemon in each jar, and give them as gifts. But if you are making the preserved lemons for your own pantry, you can use a 1-litre (1¾ pint) Kilner-style jar for storage, as the quantities given in this recipe will fill it nicely.

PRESERVED LEMONS

**MAKES ENOUGH TO FILL
5 x 250ML (9FL OZ) JARS**

330ml (11½fl oz) white wine vinegar
350ml (12fl oz) water
150g (5½oz) caster sugar
½ teaspoon sea salt
1 teaspoon black peppercorns
5 bay leaves
5 sprigs of rosemary, leaves stripped
5 large unwaxed lemons

Heat the vinegar, water and sugar together in a saucepan over a medium heat and simmer for no more than 2 minutes until the sugar has dissolved completely. Add the salt and peppercorns. Take the pan off the heat and allow the mixture to cool completely.

Put a bay leaf and the leaves from 1 sprig of rosemary into each of your sterilized jars.

Trim the ends off each lemon, then slice the lemons into sixths or eighths. Put 1 lemon slice into each jar. Divide the cooled vinegar mixture between the jars, ensuring the peppercorns are fairly evenly distributed. (If your lemons are on the small side, you may run out of liquid. If that is the case, simply top up the jars with a wee splash more of vinegar and some boiling water.) Seal the jars and store them in a dark cupboard for at least 8–10 days. The lemons will keep for up to 4 months if the jars are unopened. Once opened, store in the refrigerator and consume within 1 month.

Unlike gherkins, these are a lighter pickle with a bit more freshness from the cucumber. The booze adds a little sweetness to proceedings and means that even the biggest vinegar hater (my mother) can enjoy these. Delicious served with a selection of meats and cheeses or with burgers and salads at a barbecue.

CIDER-PICKLED CUCUMBERS

MAKES ENOUGH TO FILL 2 x 450ML (16FL OZ) JARS

5 tablespoons cider vinegar

5 tablespoons cider

50ml (2fl oz) water

50g (1¾oz) caster sugar

1 teaspoon black peppercorns

1 teaspoon sea salt

1 teaspoon yellow mustard seeds

1 large cucumber

1 very small green chilli or ½ average-sized chilli, finely sliced (deseed it if you don't want your pickle to be too spicy)

Put the vinegar, cider, water and sugar into a saucepan set over a low heat and simmer for no more than 2 minutes, until the sugar has dissolved completely. Add the peppercorns, salt and mustard seeds, then take the pan off the heat and leave the mixture to cool completely.

Trim the ends off the cucumber and cut it into pieces that are roughly as long as the height of your sterilized jars. Cut the pieces lengthways into quarters or sixths. Divide the cucumber and chilli slices between your 2 jars and pour the cooled liquid on top. Seal the jars and store in the refrigerator for 2–3 days. The pickle will keep in the refrigerator for up to 1 month.

For a sweet labneh, stir in a little honey or vanilla bean paste instead of the seasoning and olive oil and serve with granola or roasted fruits.

LABNEH

MAKES 500G (1LB 2OZ)

700ml (1¼ pints) milk
juice of ½ lemon
juice of ½ lime
salt and freshly ground black pepper
olive oil (optional)

Heat the milk and citrus juices in a heavy-based saucepan to 25°C (77°F) on a thermometer, stirring a little.

Once the liquid has reached the required temperature, take the pan off the heat and leave the liquid to cool for an hour or until you can see separation of the milk solids and liquid.

Place a doubled-up piece of muslin in a bowl and pour the milk mixture on top. Bring the edges of the muslin together snugly around the contents and tie with kitchen string. Suspend the parcel over the bowl (I tie the loose ends of the muslin to a chair or door handle and set the bowl beneath) and leave to drip for 1–2 hours or until the drips are no longer frequent and have long pauses in between. Bin the excess liquid and transfer the white curds to a clean bowl.

Beat the curds until very smooth, then season to taste with salt and pepper, and add a little olive oil, if you would like. Store in the refrigerator for up to 1 week.

Making your own nut butter is simple if you own a food processor. You can use your favourite nuts or any combination you favour, or simply use up the odds and ends of packets you find in your cupboard. And the tasty variations are endless – if making almond butter, try adding some vanilla bean paste; ground cinnamon is lovely with pecan nuts; for a seed butter, follow the same principle but use a mixture of seeds instead (pumpkin seed butter makes for delicious salad dressings); add some cocoa powder and extra sweetener in a hazelnut butter for a healthy take on Nutella. Trust me – once you've made your own, you'll never buy a nut butter again!

NUT BUTTER

**MAKES ENOUGH TO FILL
1 x 450ML (16FL OZ) JAR**

350g (12oz) nuts (you can use one
   type or a big dolly mixture)
2 tablespoons maple syrup, agave
   nectar or honey
pinch of salt

Preheat the oven to 200°C (400°F), Gas Mark 6.

Put the nuts into a roasting tray and toast them in the oven for 2 minutes. Do not let them burn!

Transfer the toasted nuts to a food processor and blitz on a high speed setting for 10 minutes, pausing to scrape down the sides of the bowl once or twice. Once the nuts have transformed into a smooth nut butter (or a nut butter of your preferred texture), add the syrup, agave or honey and a wee pinch of salt. Blitz again to incorporate the additions, then transfer the nut butter to a sterilized jar. Store in the refrigerator for a firm butter or at room temperature for a softer one. This nut butter will keep for up to 1 month.

Pour this hot salted caramel sauce over ice cream or brownies – or, as I can wholeheartedly recommend, over both together!

SALTED CARAMEL

**MAKES ENOUGH TO FILL
1 x 450ML (16FL OZ) JAR**

100g (3½oz) soft light brown sugar
100g (3½oz) caster sugar
100ml (3½fl oz) water
100g (3½oz) unsalted butter, cubed
100ml (3½fl oz) double or
 extra-thick cream
1 teaspoon vanilla bean paste
about 1 teaspoon sea salt flakes
 (such as Maldon)

In a deep saucepan, slowly melt the sugars with the water over a medium heat, stirring frequently. Once the sugars have fully dissolved, stop stirring and whack up the heat to high. Continue to cook for about 7 minutes until the liquid becomes a clear golden caramel. If it begins to crystallize at the edges, tilt the pan so that the swirling liquid dissolves the crystals a little, but do not stir.

Once the mixture achieves the right colour (watch it like a hawk, as there is nothing worse than burnt sugar), whisk in the butter cubes. When these are fully melted, take the pan off the heat and whisk in the cream and vanilla until smooth. Leave to cool for 10 minutes, then sample the sauce and add the sea salt to taste. Leave to cool completely. Transfer to a clean plastic tub and store in the refrigerator for up to 2 weeks. When required, reheat the sauce gently.

This recipe is for Gavin, a man who is obsessed with Nutella but is not so fond of its sugar content. I have tried my very best.

CHOCOLATE SPREAD

**MAKES ENOUGH TO FILL
1 x 450ML (16FL OZ) JAR**

150g (5½oz) whole blanched
 hazelnuts
250g (9oz) dark cooking chocolate
 (50–75% cocoa solids), broken
 into pieces
50g (1¾oz) caster sugar
50g (1¾oz) unsalted butter
150ml (¼ pint) hazelnut milk
150ml (¼ pint) milk
pinch of salt

Preheat the oven to 200°C (400°F), Gas Mark 6.

Put the hazelnuts in a roasting tray and toast them in the oven for 2 minutes. Transfer the toasted nuts to a food processor and blitz on high speed for 10 minutes or until it transforms into a smooth hazelnut butter. If your processor begins to overheat before the nut butter is smooth, turn it off and allow the motor to cool down, then continue to blitz the hazelnuts until they transform into a smooth spread.

Meanwhile, gently melt the chocolate in a saucepan over a low heat. Add the sugar and butter and stir until they have fully dissolved. Add the milks and the salt and continue to stir the mixture until it is completely smooth.

When the chocolate mixture is smooth, keep the motor running on the food processor and slowly pour the chocolate mixture into the smooth hazelnut butter to incorporate it. Once fully combined, transfer the mixture into a sterilized jar. Store in the refrigerator for 2–3 weeks.

Clotted cream needs to be made in a very low oven, as any higher than 60°C (140°F) and the cream will start to burn, so this recipe is not suitable for those with gas ovens.

CLOTTED CREAM

MAKES 500G (1LB 2OZ)

1.2 litres (2 pints) double cream

Preheat the oven to 60°C (140°F).

Pour the cream into a deep ceramic dish and bake for 10 hours, by which time the cream should have noticeably thickened and formed a skin on top. Transfer the dish to a wire rack and leave the mixture to cool completely.

Using a slotted spoon, carefully skim the clotted cream off the top. Place this in a clean plastic tub or sterilized glass jar. Store the clotted cream in the refrigerator for up to 5 days. (Use the excess liquid left in the base of the ceramic dish in place of milk to make luxurious pancakes or scones.)

INDEX

THANK YOU...

To you – you lovely, surprising and supportive being. Thank you for buying this book, thank you for following my very unconventional path and thank you for showing an interest in my food – it still blows my mind, and for that I am eternally grateful.

To Mumma, Daddy, Hebe and Willow. You are all barking. I love you. Mumma, thank you for your dish-washing, your sage advice in and out of the kitchen and your cuddles. Daddy, thank you for yet more dish-washing, your constructive criticism, intelligence and wit, and for (arguably the most important) the book title. Hebe, stop stealing my clothes. Thank you for your brutal honesty, your bloody great sense of humour and for keeping me down with the kids. I hope one day to be as cool as you. Willow, thank you for making me laugh time and time again, and for your endless breakfast orders. You may have been late to the party, but you are a bloomin' good addition.

To the lady behind the lens, Queen Laura Edwards. You have a magic vision and I cannot tell you how much I adore every single one of your images. One million times thank you. You made this a reality, and a very pretty one at that.

To Tabitha Hawkins. The most energetic, entertaining and excellent lady I have had the good fortune of knowing. I love both your work and your zumba dancing, and I am eternally grateful for your props and presence.

To Annie Rigg. The work you put into this project still renders me speechless. Your ability to make food both striking and delicate was thrilling to watch. Thank you for feeding us, fuelling us and keeping us smiling. I am heartbroken that the glasses picture didn't make the cut.

To Kendal Noctor, April Carter, Lola Milne and Emily Jonzen. You are all, as I like to say, "a wee bit fab". Also special thanks to Kendal for not jumping into Rumbling Bridge the night before our Scotland shoot, and to April for cooking your socks off at seven months pregnant – little Ada is simply gorgeous. All of your efforts have not gone unnoticed.

To Jaz Bahra. You just got it. Thank you for executing everything so beautifully and thank you for listening to my constant chatter, nonsense ideas and driving *that* car when we were in Scotland.

To Eleanor Maxfield and everyone who has worked so hard at Octopus. Huge thanks for even agreeing to meet me in the first place. I am so honoured to have been taken under your wing, and even more thrilled to have had such a good time along the way. You are all a truly amazing bunch.

To Heather Holden-Brown, Jack Munnelly and Cara Armstrong. I couldn't have done anything without you all standing beside me and cheering me on. Thank you for your constant, endless and much-needed support.

To my exceptional and unbelievably good-looking team *Gatherings*: Kirsty Fisher, Megan Lancaster, Emma Cox, Hannah Fisher, Lauren Blakeborough and angel Alice, Hebe Shedden, Willow Shedden, Ruby Flatley, Alex Beard, Georgina Webster, Julia Cox, James Irvine, Mat Riley, Calum Tait, Sorren Maclean, Niall McIntosh, Scott Alcorn, Hector Lancaster, Jamie Yellowlees and Andrew Mathieson. Also big thank you to Grandpa Kenneth, Granny Joan, Uncle Gav, Auntie Annie, Una and Chrissie the cutest cousins a lady could ask for, Auntie Trish, Uncle Michael, Iona Lancaster, Andrea Cox, Mags Quigley, Steph Hand and Maggie Hand. Everyone of you has all helped me more than you could ever know. I love you all. Thank you, thank you, thank you.

To my bonnie bonnie home turf, Dunkeld and Birnam. To Cat and Alex at Eastwood House – thank you for letting us run wild on the banks of the Tay, and letting us shoot in the most stunning location. I couldn't have asked for more. To everyone at Birnam Arts – your constant support (10 years of it!) has been so so valuable. Thank you for letting me set up camp for over a month, and for playing me Springsteen during the long writing process. To Fi and Charlie Cameron at Xmas Direct – you know how much I love a fairy light! Thank you for your generosity. To Heather "salad" Hamilton – thank you for your lovely leaves! To Kevin Lancaster – thank you for helping us out in the pissing rain minutes before Bonfire Night was due to commence! To Hugh and Julie Goring and everyone at Frames Gallery in Perth – thank you for everything. I look back so fondly on my time with you all, and doubt anything would be as it is without you.

And finally, a special thank you to Diana Henry, who despite having never met me has provided endless advice (even when I emailed you at 1am), generosity and general presence during my route into the wild and fantastical foodie world. Your recipes encouraged me to get into the kitchen and I am constantly inspired by your cooking, which I would argue is the most creative and comforting of all.